C I T Y P A C K
London

By Louise Nicholson

Fodor's

Fodor's Travel Publications, Inc.
New York • Toronto • London • Sydney • Auckland

Page 1: Household Cavalry
guardsman, Horse Guards

Page 2: Hampton Court
Palace

Page 5 (a): commissionaire,
Bank of England
Page 5 (b): flower seller,
Covent Garden Piazza

Page 13 (a): The Old Bell
pub sign, Fleet Steet
Page 13 (b): Beefeater,
H.M. The Tower of London

Page 23 (a): St. Paul's
Cathedral
Page 23 (b): Nelson's
Column, Trafalgar Square

Page 49 (a): The Lloyds
Building, in the City
Page 49 (b): Statue of Eros,
Piccadilly Circus

Page 87 (a): Piccadilly
Circus
Page 87 (b): mailbox

Published in the United States by Fodor's Travel
Publications, Inc.
Published in the United Kingdom by AA Publishing

Fodor's is a trademark of Fodor's Travel Publications, Inc.

ISBN 0–679–02958–3
First Edition

Fodor's Citypack London

Author: Louise Nicholson
Cartography: The Automobile Association
           RV Reise- und Verkehrsverlag
Cover Design: Tigist Getachew, Fabrizio La Rocca

Special Sales

Color separation by Daylight Colour Art Pte Ltd, Singapore
Manufactured by Dai Nippon Printing Co. (Hong Kong) Ltd

10 9 8 7 6 5 4 3

Contents

About this book

Citypack London is divided into six sections to cover the six most important aspects of your visit to London.

1. LONDON LIFE *(pages 5–12)*
Your personal introduction to London by author Louise Nicholson
    Facts and figures
    Leading characters
    The big events in London's history

2. HOW TO ORGANIZE YOUR TIME *(pages 13–22)*
Make the most of your time in London
    4 one-day itineraries
    2 suggested walks
    2 evening strolls
    4 excursions beyond the city

3. LONDON'S TOP 25 SIGHTS *(pages 23–48)*
Your concise guide to sightseeing
    Louise Nicholson's choice, with her personal introduction to each sight
    Description and history
    Highlights of each attraction
    Practical information
    Each sight located on the inside cover of the book

4. LONDON'S BEST *(pages 49–60)*
What London is renowned for
    Museums & Galleries
    House Museums
    Statues & Monuments
    Modern Buildings
    Churches & Cathedrals
    Green Spaces
    Thames Sights
    Children's Favorites
    Hidden London

5. LONDON: WHERE TO... *(pages 61–86)*
The best places to eat, shop, be entertained and stay
    14 categories of restaurants
    8 categories of store
    5 categories of entertainment venues
    3 categories of hotels
    Price bands and reservation details

6. LONDON TRAVEL FACTS *(pages 87–94)*
Essential information for your stay

SYMBOLS

Throughout the guide a few straightforward symbols are used to denote the following categories:

➕ map reference on the fold-out map accompanying this book (see below)

✉ address

☎ telephone number

🕐 opening times

🍴 restaurant or café on premises or nearby

Ⓜ nearest underground train station

🚆 nearest overground train station

🚢 nearest riverboat stop

♿ facilities for visitors with disabilities

🎟 admission charge

↔ other places of interest nearby

❓ tours, lectures or special events

➤ page where you will find a fuller description

MAPS

All map references are to the separate fold-out map accompanying this book. For example, the Wallace Collection, in Manchester Square, has the following information: ➕ E5 – indicating the grid square of the map in which the Wallace Collection will be found. All entries within the Top 25 Sights section are also plotted by number (not page number) on the city-center map located on the inside front and back covers of this book.

PRICES

Where appropriate, an indication of the cost of an establishment is given by £ signs: £££ denotes higher prices, ££ denotes average praices, while £ denotes lower charges.

LONDON
life

A PERSONAL VIEW

Some people claim they know London. They cannot possibly. For me, the joy of this city is that it can never be known. After 20 years here, I am still a beginner, familiar with some parts, baffled by others.

The stimulus of London is that there is always somewhere left to explore, something new to learn, some dynamic change afoot. Just when I think I have got to grips with it, the great city surprises and confronts me, turning all assumptions upside-down. A view will be changed by a new building, like the one across the river from Greenwich after the arrival of the shining shaft of Canary Wharf Tower. Familiar pictures will disappear, at the annual rehang in the Tate Gallery for example, and a feast of new canvases will come into view. Whole areas will change their mood, as Soho has done since the mid-1980s, its friendly seediness transformed into squeaky-clean trendiness.

Canary Wharf and Canary Wharf Tower, Docklands

London is a fast city. It buzzes by day and night. Londoners tend to be busy, in a rush, independent. What for them is the enjoyable anonymity of a city can be tough for visitors to deal with, particularly since the climate does not encourage a café society for much of the year. But take a deep breath and join in London life at London's pace, and you will find that we are much more friendly than expected.

London is also an expensive city. But Londoners know how to get the most out of it—from the parks, the churches with free music, the great free national museums, and traditional events

with their parades and colors, to Travelcards, plenty of cheap theater deals, and much, much more. London on a budget need not restrict you.

London is in an administrative muddle. For a city which was once the powerful capital of an efficiently run empire stretching round the world, London today is in an astounding mess. It has no central city administration, no properly coordinated public transportation, and too many cars. And yet London has its own order. This city is rare in being truly cosmopolitan and the political, economic and cultural capital of the country. Its citizens share the rhythm of the seasons in the great parks. They share in the annual round of tradition and culture. I still walk in St. James's Park at daffodil time, line up for cheap concert tickets at the Proms, and join Italians at their July festival in Clerkenwell.

London has it all, whatever you want. Simply take London and make of it what you wish.

A floodlit Tower Bridge silhouettes the Waterfall *sculpture in Tower Bridge Piazza*

The Thames

"The old river on its broad reach unrolled at the decline of day, after ages of good service done to the race that people its bank, spread out in the tranquil dignity of a waterway leading to the uttermost ends of the earth ... What greatness had not floated on the ebb of that river into the mystery of an unknown earth ... the dreams of men, the seed of commonwealth, the germs of empires."

— Joseph Conrad, *Heart of Darkness*

LONDON IN FIGURES

CITY SITE
- The capital of England and Great Britain, founded by the Romans in A.D. 43 as a trading port on the River Thames, 40 miles inland from the North Sea.

- London is really two cities. The City of London has its origins in the Roman port and is still the commercial center. The City of Westminster, founded a thousand years later 2½ miles upstream, has always been the royal, political and religious center.

GREEN PLACES
- Greater London covers 625 square miles, of which 11 percent comprises 1,700 parks.

LANGUAGES & NATIONALITIES
- Londoners speak between them almost 200 languages. About 30 percent were born elsewhere. English is the predominant language, followed by Bengali and then Turkish, Chinese, Gujerati, Urdu, Punjabi, Arabic, and Spanish.

ECONOMY
- London's principal industries are retailing, the public sector and tourism, followed by banking, insurance, transportation, communications, and manufacturing.

TOURISTS
- There are 10.7 million overseas and 8 million British visitors to London a year.

- The top attractions are the British Museum, the National Gallery, Westminster Abbey, Madame Tussaud's, and the Tower of London.

POPULATION
- During the 16th century London was Europe's fastest growing city, the population rising from 75,000 to 200,000.

- By 1700 London was Europe's biggest and wealthiest city, with about 700,000 people.

- London continued to grow, from under 1 million in 1800 to 6.5 million by 1900, peaking in the 1930s and 1940s at 10 million.

- The population has now fallen to 6.8 million.

LONDON PEOPLE

SIR NORMAN FOSTER

Foster's avid love of flying anything from sailplanes to light aircraft gives him a bird's-eye view of buildings old and new. Architect of the Sackler Galleries at the Royal Academy, Stansted Airport, and several other London buildings, Norman Foster trained in Britain and the U.S. and has designed award-winning buildings all over the world. It was Foster and Partners who created the redevelopment plan for the King's Cross area, and it is they who will transform the British Museum once the British Library is relocated there.

SIR TERENCE CONRAN

Synonymous with the shopping revolution of the 1970s, when he founded the Habitat chain, Conran remains a pioneer. His Conran stores sell good design at affordable prices. He has also opened a clutch of successful restaurants. The heart of Conran's empire is Butler's Wharf, where the Blue Print café sits above his Design Museum, near another three restaurants and a food hall.

FRANK BRUNO

Franklin Roy Bruno began his boxing career with the Wandsworth Boys Club in 1970 when he was nine. He turned professional in 1982, has had over 30 victories and finally, on his thrid attempt, claimed a world heavyweight title in 1995, defeating American Oliver McCall in London. His bluff and down-to-earth sense of humor has won him a place in the affections of the capital, and he has acted in children's theater and on TV.

VIVIENNE WESTWOOD

Britain's brightest and whackiest clothes designer maintains a prominent place in the fashion avant-garde. While in the King's Road, she created punk street style, but after fashion shows such as "Witches and Hypnos" she moved upmarket to Mayfair. Here she continues to be crazily imaginative, called her 1995 collection "Erotic Zones," and despite claims to anarchy, has entered the staid pages of *Who's Who.*

The Governor of H.M. The Tower of London

The Governor of H.M. The Tower of London lives in a house on Tower Green and is in local command of the Tower and its 150 or so residents. The current Governor, Major General Geoffrey Field, will oversee the refurbishment of the White Tower and the extension of the Wall Walk, perhaps outstripping his predecessor, who increased the Tower's income by two thirds and visitors by 10 percent.

Vivienne Westwood

9

A CHRONOLOGY

A.D. 43	Emperor Claudius invades Britain; a deep-water port, Londinium, is soon established.
200	The Romans put a wall around Londinium, now capital of Britannia Superior; they withdraw in 410.
1042	Edward the Confessor becomes king, making London capital of England and Westminster his home; begins the abbey-church of St. Peter.
1066	The Norman king, William the Conqueror, defeats King Harold at the Battle of Hastings; begins the Tower of London.
1176	Peter de Colechurch builds London's first stone bridge, London Bridge.
1477	William Caxton publishes the first book printed in England, on his presses at Westminster.
1485	Tudor rule begins, ending 1603; London is Europe's fastest growing city.
1529	Cardinal Thomas Wolsey fails to win Henry VIII a divorce and falls from favor.
1531	Inigo Jones designs London's first square, Covent Garden Piazza.
1533	Henry VIII breaks with Rome to marry Anne Boleyn; establishes the Church of England.
1649	Charles I is executed in Whitehall; the Commonwealth (1649–53) and Protectorate (1653–59) govern England until Charles II is restored to the throne in 1660.
1666	The Great Fire of London. Sir Christopher Wren begins St. Paul's Cathedral in 1675.
1694	William Paterson founds the Bank of England to fund William and Mary's war with France.
1700	London becomes Europe's biggest and wealthiest city; population 700,000.

1759	The British Museum, London's first public museum, opens.
1800–1900	London's population grows from 1 to 6.5 million; 14 Thames bridges built 1811–17 and 15 railroad stations 1836–74.
1802	London becomes the world's largest port.
1816–28	John Nash lays out Regent Street, Regent's Park and Regent's Canal.
1829	Sir Robert Peel establishes the Metropolitan Police force; a horse-drawn bus service begins.
1834	The Palace of Westminster burns down; the new building is almost complete in 1847; the Clock Tower ("Big Ben") is finished in 1858.
1837	Queen Victoria begins her 64-year-long reign.
1851	The Great Exhibition is held in Hyde Park.
1863	World's first urban underground train service, the Metropolitan Railway, opens. In 1890 the first Tube train runs on the Northern Line.
1922	First daily wireless (radio) program broadcast from Savoy Hill; B.B.C. established 1927, first broadcasts in 1936 from Alexandra Palace.
1939–45	Blitz bombings destroy a third of the City of London and much of the docks.
1951	Festival of Britain held on the site of the South Bank arts complex.
1960s	The Beatles, Carnaby Street and the King's Road help create "swinging London."
1980s	As a result of post-war conservation movements, 30,000 London buildings and 300 London areas are now protected by law.
1981	Government-backed London Docklands Development Corporation (LDDC) begins the revitalization of the docklands.
1994	First Eurostar trains travel through the Channel Tunnel between London and Paris.

PEOPLE & EVENTS FROM HISTORY

Statue of Boudicca on Westminster Bridge

SIR HUGH MYDDELTON
The statue of a Tudor aristocrat in doublet and hose stands on Islington Green. This is Sir Hugh Myddelton, a wealthy Welsh goldsmith who became jeweler to James I. Recognizing the lack of good fresh water in the city, he cut a channel from the River Lea, 40 miles away in Hertfordshire, which brought fresh water directly into London —for which he was rewarded with a baronetcy.

SIR JOSEPH BAZALGETTE
As London grew, so did the sewage pouring into the Thames, until in summer it was known as the Great Stink. Bazalgette solved the problem by building the 3½-mile Victoria Embankment (1864–74). It incorporates a trunk sewer, underground railroad and flood wall, and is topped by a road, riverside walk and Embankment Gardens.

JOHN NASH
John Nash created theatrical, stucco-fronted architectural designs. From 1811 onwards, backed by the Prince Regent (later George IV), he gave London its first large-scale unified plan. The great sweep of Regent Street from St. James's Park through Portland Place to Regent's Park emulated Paris in its order and grandeur.

QUEEN BOUDICCA
In A.D. 62, when the widowed Boudicca, Queen of the Iceni in Norfolk, found herself insulted, dispossessed and flogged by the Roman Procurator, she and her people revolted. They sacked Colchester, then marched on London while its governor was away. The thriving city was plundered and laid waste. In 1902 Thomas Thorneycroft immortalized the heroine Queen and her daughters in his bronze on Westminster Bridge.

The Great Fire of London
The fire that broke out at a baker's near Pudding Lane on the night of September 2nd, 1666, was the worst of many fires around that time. Raging for four days and nights, it destroyed four-fifths of the City and 13,200 homes. Sir Christopher Wren, grand architect of the consequent rebuilding of London, designed St. Paul's Cathedral, 51 churches (23 still stand), and the Monument to the tragic fire.

LONDON
how to organize your time

13

ITINERARIES

Walking is the best way to get under London's skin. Using the map, select an area and simply explore. Here are four ideas—but do wander off down an alleyway or into an old shop or a church if you see something intriguing.

ITINERARY ONE	EARLY LONDON: THE CITY
	It is best to walk around the City on a weekday.
Breakfast	Hearty breakfast at a Smithfield pub (➤ 64)
Morning	St. Bartholomew-the-Great (➤ 46)
	Walk through the medieval side streets to the Museum of London (➤ 47)
	Roman wall in the Barbican and Noble Street
	Goldsmith's Hall and Foster Lane
	Walk along Cheapside, down Bow Lane and left up Queen Victoria Street
Lunch	Lunch at Sweetings seafood restaurant (➤ 63)
Afternoon	Temple of Mithras, Bucklersbury (➤ 60)
	St. Margaret, Lothbury (➤ 55)
	Guildhall: huge medieval crypt, Clockmakers' Company clocks (Mon–Fri 9–5)
ITINERARY TWO	CHIC LONDON: ST. JAMES'S
	Especially good for art galleries; best Mon–Fri.
Morning	Jermyn Street (➤ 70), then St. James's Square and into King Street (Spinks and Christies ➤ 72)
	St. James's Palace, where the Changing of the Guard begins (➤ 22)
	Up St. James's Street and into St. James's Place to Spencer House (open Sun only, not Jan, Aug)
	Through the tunnel to Queen's Walk by Green Park (➤ 56). Stop for a picnic lunch or:
Lunch	Tavola Calda at Café Torino, 189 Piccadilly
Afternoon	Walk along Piccadilly, delving into the Ritz, Fortnum & Mason and Hatchards (➤ 76)
	St. James's Church (➤ 55)
	The Royal Academy (➤ 51)
	Through Burlington Arcade to the Museum of Mankind (➤ 51)
	Bond Street New and Old (➤ 70), Cork Street

ITINERARIES

ITINERARY THREE	ROYAL LONDON

Choose a dry day on which to alternate parks and picnics with palaces and palatial houses.

Morning
Kensington Palace and Kensington
Gardens (➤ 25)
Hyde Park (➤ 56)
Apsley House (➤ 52)
Green Park (➤ 56)
Buckingham Palace (➤ 32) (Queen's Gallery is
the most likely part to be open)

Lunch
Picnic lunch in St. James's Park (➤ 33)

Afternoon
Horse Guards through to Banqueting
House (➤ 37)
Parliament Square, filled with statues of past
prime ministers
The Houses of Parliament (➤ 36)
Westminster Abbey, where there may be
afternoon Evensong (➤ 35)

ITINERARY FOUR	LONDON, CAPITAL OF AN EMPIRE

You will need to use some public transportation on this walk.

Morning
St. Paul's Cathedral (➤ 45): public statues and
memorials in St. Paul's and the streets around.
Take bus no. 11, 15, or 23 to Trafalgar Square,
dedicated to Nelson and sea heroes (➤ 53)
National Portrait Gallery (➤ 38)
Walk down The Mall, laid out as a processional
route for Queen Victoria. There's a triumphal
arch at one end and her memorial at the other,
set in a circle symbolizing the Empress at the
heart of her empire

Lunch
Dip into St. James's Park for lunch (➤ 33)

Afternoon
Take the Underground (District and Circle line)
from St. James's Park to Kensington High Street
or the no. 9 bus from Trafalgar Square via Hyde
Park Corner to Kensington High Street
Pay a visit to the museum in artist Linley
Sambourne's former home, 8 Stafford
Terrace, or in Leighton House (➤ 52)

WALKS

THE SIGHTS

- Tower Bridge Museum (➤ 57)
- Design Museum (➤ 50–1)
- Bramah Tea and Coffee Museum, Clove Building, Maguire Street, SE1 ☎ 0171-378 0222
- H.M.S. *Belfast* (➤ 58)
- The London Dungeon (➤ 58)
- The Clink Exhibition, 1 Clink Street, SE1, ☎ 0171-403 6515
- Shakespeare Globe Museum, New Globe Walk, Bankside, SE1, ☎ 0171-928 6406
- South Bank Arts Complex (➤ 11, 51, and 80)

INFORMATION

Distance approx 1½ miles
Time 2–3 hours, depending on indoor visits
Start point Tower Bridge
🚇 K6
🚉 Tower Hill
End point Royal Festival Hall, South Bank
🚇 G6
🚉 Waterloo
🚆 Waterloo

THE SOUTH BANK: THE DESIGN MUSEUM TO WESTMINSTER BRIDGE

This walk hugs the bank of the Thames and enjoys superb views across London's core on the north bank. Begin at Tower Bridge Museum, for high-level London views. Then stroll eastwards among the old warehouses and new restaurants of Shad Thames to find Anthony Donaldson's *Waterfall* sculpture in Tower Bridge Piazza, Piers Gough's dramatic *The Circle*, the riverfront Design Museum on Butler's Wharf, and the Bramah Tea and Coffee Museum behind.

West of Tower Bridge, the path leads to H.M.S. *Belfast* and Hay's Galleria for more cafés. The London Dungeon lies behind. Outside the Cottons Centre is a pavilion where a map plots the buildings along the City view. Over London Bridge is Southwark Cathedral, the Clink Exhibition, and a wall and rose window of the 14th-century Winchester Palace's Great Hall.

Between Southwark and Blackfriars bridges is the Shakespeare Globe Museum and Bankside Power Station (soon to be a Tate Gallery outpost). The riverfront widens at the South Bank Arts Complex, offering exhibitions, cafés, and performances. Hungerford footbridge leads to Charing Cross; Westminster Bridge to Westminster.

16

Monument (1408) to poet John Gower, Southwark Cathedral

WALKS

THE TWO CITIES: CITY OF WESTMINSTER TO THE CITY OF LONDON

The heart of Westminster is still Westminster Abbey and the Houses of Parliament—there is a good view of the riverfront from the south end of Westminster Bridge.

From statue-filled Parliament Square (with a diagram of who's who on the east side), Whitehall leads up past Downing Street—official home of the Prime Minister—Horse Guards, and Banqueting House, to Trafalgar Square, home of the National Gallery. The National Portrait Gallery is at the end of St. Martin's Lane. Farther on, past the Coliseum, turn right through New Row into Covent Garden, a good place to stop for refreshment. On the Piazza, find the London Transport Museum and, nearby, the Theatre Museum. Down on the Strand, turn left and go through Aldwych to the Courtauld Institute Galleries on the south side.

In Fleet Street, winged dragons mark the boundary of the City of London and Westminster. Just before the junction with Chancery Lane, an alley on the right leads to Temple Church and the Inner and Middle Inns. Farther on, Johnson's Court (between nos. 166 and 167) leads to Dr. Johnson's House on the left, while St. Bride's is on the right, tucked behind the Reuters building. St. Paul's Cathedral stands at the top of Ludgate Hill. Behind it, Watling Street leads to Bow Lane and a choice of places for lunch or for dinner.

THE SIGHTS

- Westminster Bridge
- Houses of Parliament (➤ 36)
- Westminster Abbey (➤ 35)
- Parliament Square
- Whitehall
- Downing Street
- Horse Guards
- Banqueting House (➤ 37)
- National Gallery (➤ 39)
- National Portrait Gallery (➤ 38)
- Coliseum (➤ 80)
- Covent Garden (➤ 40)
- London Transport Museum (➤ 40)
- Strand
- Courtauld Institute Galleries (➤ 41)
- Fleet Street
- Temple Church (➤ 55)
- Inns of Court (➤ 60)
- Dr. Johnson's House (➤ 52)
- St. Bride's Church
- St. Paul's Cathedral (➤ 45)
- Bow Lane

INFORMATION

Distance 2–2½ miles
Time 3–6 hours, depending on museum and church visits
Start point Westminster Bridge
⊞ G6
◉ Westminster
End point Bow Street
⊞ G5
◉ Mansion House

Statue of 2nd Duke of Cambridge (1819–1904), by Adrian Jones, in Whitehall 17

EVENING STROLLS

London is gently lit by street-lights, neon signs and the occasional floodlight, nothing very dramatic. Look for the surviving gas lamps. Both of the following strolls end in Soho, the heart of night-time London.

INFORMATION

Royal & Aristocratic Evocations
Distance ½ mile
Time 30–40 minutes
Start point Buckingham Palace
➕ F6
🚇 Green Park, St. James's Park and Victoria
End point Piccadilly Circus
➕ F5
🚇 Piccadilly Circus

The Political Path
Distance ½ mile
Time 40 minutes–1 hour
Start point Westminster Bridge
➕ G6
🚇 Westminster
End point Shaftesbury Avenue
➕ F5–G5
🚇 Piccadilly Circus and Leicester Square

Shaftesbury Avenue

ROYAL & ARISTOCRATIC EVOCATIONS
Buckingham Palace's gray Portland stone has a more fairytale quality at night. In front of it glints the Queen Victoria Memorial, while St. James's Park fountains sparkle under floodlights.

Marlborough Road leads from The Mall to Pall Mall, where gas flares may illuminate an old club's façade. The red brick of St. James's Palace glows warmly, and old gas lamps shed a gentle light on the lanes behind it and to the left up St. James's Street. Along Piccadilly, Piccadilly Circus's neon lights and Eros statue are the gateway to Shaftesbury Avenue's theaters and Soho's nightlife.

THE POLITICAL PATH
From Westminster Bridge, enjoy close-ups of the Houses of Parliament and gilded Big Ben, and distant views along the twisting Thames to St. Paul's Cathedral and the City. In Parliament Square and up Whitehall, spot who was who in the statues of London's heroes and villains.

Lutyens's fountains splash at the foot of Nelson's illuminated column in Trafalgar Square; other naval stars surround him. Up behind the National Gallery, Leicester Square's great movie theaters dwarf the crowds of visitors and the occasional street musician. Chinese Soho, perfumed by its many fine restaurants, fills the lanes north of here to Shaftesbury Avenue, the focus being Gerrard Street (pedestrians only; no cars).

ORGANIZED SIGHTSEEING

Taking a guided tour is a good way to enjoy a London panorama and gain in-depth information from a Londoner. Walking tours get deeper into London life. They have good leaders, last about two hours, are cheap and do not need to be booked in advance. Bus tours have various pick-up points, including at some hotels.

See also the Thames (➤ 57), National Theatre (➤ 78–79), Wembley Stadium (➤ 83).

EVAN EVANS
Blue Badge guides for walks (for example, Jack the Ripper), river cruises, and out-of-town tours.
✉ 26 Cockspur Street, Trafalgar Square, SW1 ☎ 0181-332 2222

FRAMES RICKARDS
Blue Badge guides for general, evening, thematic (ghosts, etc.) and out-of-town tours.
✉ 11 Herbrand Street, WC1 ☎ 0171-837 3111

THE ORIGINAL LONDON WALKS
The Tuckers organize a walk for most days of the year, guided by enthusiasts and experts.
✉ P O Box 1708, NW6 ☎ 0171-624 3978

THE ORIGINAL LONDON SIGHTSEEING TOUR
Taped commentary (eight languages) for the tour; live commentary for London Plus.
✉ London Coaches, Jews Road, SW18 ☎ 0181-877 1722

TAKE-A-GUIDE
Tailor-made tours by foot or car.
✉ 11 Uxbridge Street, W8 ☎ 0181-857 1545

BUS TRIP TO MURDER
The "hit list" includes Jack the Ripper and Sweeney Todd on this evening tour lasting 3½ hours; reservations a must.
✉ Tragical History Tours ☎ 0181-857 1545

THE BIG BUS COMPANY
Live commentary on the maroon and cream, mostly open-topped, double decker buses; Panoramic and Stopper tours (hop-on hop-off).
✉ Waterside Way, SW17 ☎ 0181-944 7810

Buildings and more buildings
With London's quantity and quality of architecture, all sorts of societies organize tours to look at it. Architectural Dialogue (0181-341 1371) have Sat. morning and other tours led by architects and architectural historians. The Georgian Group (0171-377 1722), Victorian Society (0181-994 1019) and Twentieth Century Society (0171-250 3857) all do walks and tours, too. To see new Docklands buildings, the LDDC Visitors Centre (0171-512 1111) will suggest a guide.

Guardsman, St. James's Palace

19

EXCURSIONS

INFORMATION

Greenwich

Distance 4 miles from London
Bridge and Tower Hill, 5
miles from Westminster
Bridge

Journey time 20 mins–1 hour

🚆 Docklands Light Railway to
Island Gardens, then foot
tunnel

🚢 Riverboat from Westminster,
Charing Cross or Tower piers

National Maritime Museum

✉ Romney Road, SE10

☎ 0181-858 4422

🕐 Mon–Sat 10–6, Sun 12–6
(winter daily until 5)

♿ Very expensive

Greenwich Tourist Information

✉ 46 Greenwich Church Street,
Greenwich, SE10

☎ 0181-858 6376

🕐 Daily

Hampton Court

Distance Approx 11 miles

Journey time 30 mins by train,
3–4 hours by boat

🚆 Waterloo railroad station to
Hampton Court

🚢 Riverboat from Westminster
Pier

Hampton Court Palace

✉ East Molesey, Surrey

☎ 0181-781 9500

🕐 Tue–Sun 9:30–6, Mon
10:15–6

♿ Very expensive

GREENWICH

Downstream from the City lies Greenwich. At its core is a favorite royal palace, the Queen's House, designed by Inigo Jones, which is surrounded by the Royal Naval College (formerly the Royal Naval Hospital), designed by Christopher Wren. Go early and for the whole day. There is plenty to see, plus markets and craft fairs on the weekends (▶ 74).

The National Maritime Museum, the world's largest nautical museum, fills the old Royal Hospital School and incorporates Queen's House. Up the hill is the Old Royal Observatory —the Greenwich Meridian (0° longitude), passes through here. Nearby, the hilltop terrace provides London's grandest view; behind lie the Ranger's House and the Fan Museum. Before you leave, see the Painted Hall and Chapel inside Wren's Hospital, and two special boats: the *Cutty Sark* and *Gipsy Moth IV*.

HAMPTON COURT PALACE

This is London's most impressive royal palace, well worth the journey west out of the city center. When King Henry VIII dismissed Cardinal Wolsey in 1529, he took over his already ostentatious Tudor palace and enlarged it. Successive monarchs altered and repaired both the palace and its 60 acres of Tudor and baroque gardens.

The best way to visit this huge collection of chambers, courtyards, and state apartments is to follow one of the six clearly indicated routes— perhaps Henry VIII's State Apartments or the King's Apartments built for William III, immaculately restored after a devastating fire. Outside, do not miss the Tudor gardens, the Maze, and other restored gardens, where there are guided historical walks each afternoon.

WINDSOR

The fairytale towers and turrets of Windsor Castle make this the ultimate queen's castle—it is indeed an official residence of the Queen and

EXCURSIONS

her Court. It was begun by William the Conqueror, rebuilt in stone by Henry II, and there have been embellishments ever since. Various parts are open; if the State Apartments and St. George's Chapel are closed, there is still plenty to see. Changing of the Guard at 11AM.

Outside the castle lie Windsor's pretty, medieval cobblestone lanes, Christopher Wren's Guildhall, and the delightful Theatre Royal. Beyond it, you can explore Windsor Great Park's 4,800 acres with their stunning views, or cross the Thames to Eton.

AN ADAM DOUBLE: SYON & OSTERLEY

To use public transportation and see both houses, do this trip on a Saturday.

Two magnificent country mansions and their parks lie southwest of London. At each, with meticulous attention to detail both inside and out, Robert Adam transformed a 16th-century house into an elegant neo-classical mansion.

Osterley is a rare example of a well-preserved house and 140-acre park close to London. First completed in 1575, Adam's transformation in 1760–80 was for the banker Robert Child. Thameside Syon is even more sumptuous. Its opulent furnishings were made for Hugh Smithson, 1st Duke of Northumberland, whose family still owns Syon. Don't miss the Conservatory or London Butterfly House.

Syon House

INFORMATION

Windsor
Distance 17 miles
Journey time 35–50 mins
🚉 Waterloo or Paddington

Windsor Castle
☎ 01753 868286, x 2235
🕐 Apr–Oct 10–5; Nov–Mar 10–4
💷 Very expensive

Windsor Tourist Information
✉ 24 High Street, Windsor
☎ 01753 852010
🕐 Mon–Sat 9:30–5, Sun 10–5

Syon & Osterley
Distance 9 miles
Journey time 1 hour to either
🚇 Piccadilly line to Osterley; then bus H28, H91 to Syon. From Syon, bus 237, 267 to Kew Bridge to Waterloo.

Syon House
✉ Brentford, Middlesex
☎ 0181-560 0881/2/3
🕐 House Apr–Sep, Sat, Sun, holidays 11–5; Oct, Sun 11–5. Park 10–6 or dusk
🍴 Café
💷 Expensive

Osterley Park
✉ Isleworth, Middlesex
☎ 0181-560 3918
🕐 House Apr–Oct, Wed–Sat 1–5, Sun, holidays 11–5. Closed Good Fri. Park 9–7:30 or dusk
🍴 Café
💷 Moderate

WHAT'S ON

London's festivals and traditions provide free, colorful events and are often the chance to see buildings usually closed to the public. The London Tourist Board publishes a free festivals booklet; most are in the weekly listings in the magazine *Time Out*.

JANUARY	*The sales* (most of Jan): shopping bargains
FEBRUARY	*Chinese New Year* (end of Feb): dragon dances and firecrackers in Soho
MARCH	*Chelsea Antiques Fair* (Mar 5–17): Chelsea Old Town Hall
APRIL	*Oxford and Cambridge Boat Race* (1st Saturday): Putney to Mortlake on the Thames *London Marathon* (1st Sunday): the world's biggest
MAY	*Chelsea Flower Show* (end of May): one of the world's best, at the Royal Hospital, Chelsea
JUNE	*Trooping the Colour* (2nd Saturday): the "Colours" (flags) are trooped before the Queen on Horseguards Parade, Whitehall *Wimbledon* (end of June): the world's leading tennis tournament
JULY	*Promenade Concerts—"The Proms"* (Jul and Aug): a series of classical concerts in the Albert Hall
AUGUST	*Notting Hill Carnival* (last weekend, Bank Holiday Monday): Europe's biggest
SEPTEMBER	*Election of the Lord Mayor of London* (Sep 29): the Lord Mayor and his successor-elect ride in the state coach to the Mansion House
OCTOBER	*Cockney Harvest Festival Supper* (1st Sunday): traditional "Pearly Kings and Queens" clothing at St. Martins-in-the-Fields
NOVEMBER	*Bonfire Night* (Nov 5): fires and fireworks commemorate the failed "Gunpowder Plot" of 1605
DECEMBER	*Christmas Tree* (mid-month): the annual gift from Norway is raised in Trafalgar Square
DAILY	*The Changing of the Guard*: At St James's Palace, Guards march to Buckingham Palace at 11.15, returning at 12.10; at Buckingham Palace, the Guard is changed at 11:30 on alternate days; at Horse Guards, by the former Whitehall Palace, at 11 on alternate weekdays, Sun at 10; at Windsor Castle, at 11 on alternate weekdays [winter] or daily [summer], (never on Sun). The ceremonies are cancelled in very bad weather. ☎ 0839 123411 for current information.

LONDON's
top 25 sights

The sights are numbered from west to east across the city

1

ROYAL BOTANICAL GARDENS, KEW

HIGHLIGHTS

- Arriving by riverboat
- Kew Palace and garden
- Gallery walks, Palm House
- Temperate House (see below)
- Springtime woods and dells
- Oak Avenue to Queen Charlotte's Cottage
- The rose pergola

INFORMATION

- ✉ Kew Road, Kew, Richmond
- ☎ 0181-332 5000
- 🕐 Daily 9:30AM–dusk. Closed Dec 25, Jan 1
- 🍴 Good
- 🚇 Kew Gardens
- 🚉 Kew Bridge
- ♿ Excellent
- 🚹 Moderate
- ↔ Syon House (➤21)
- ❓ Guided tours 11 and 2; jazz concerts 3rd week July

The Princess of Wales Conservatory

Whether the trees are shrouded in winter mists, the azaleas are bursting with blossoms or the lawns are dotted with summer picnickers reading Sunday newspapers, Kew never fails to work its magic on me.

Royal beginnings The 300-acre gardens containing 44,000 different plants and many glorious greenhouses make up the world's foremost botanical research center. But it began modestly. George III's mother, Princess Augusta, planted just 9 acres in 1759, helped by gardener William Aiton and botanist Lord Bute. Architect Sir William Chambers built the Pagoda, Orangery, Ruined Arch, and three temples. Later, George III enlarged the gardens to their present size and invited Sir Joseph Banks (head gardener 1772–1819), who had traveled with Captain Cook, to plant them with specimens from all over the world.

Victorian order When the gardens were given to the nation in 1841, Sir William Hooker became director for 24 years. He founded the Department of Economic Botany, the museums, the Herbarium, and the Library, while W. A. Nesfield laid out the lake, pond, and the four great vistas: Pagoda Vista, Broad Walk, Holly Walk, and Cedar Vista.

The greenhouses Chambers' Orangery is now the Gardens' shop and restaurant. To see plant-filled greenhouses, seek out Decimus Burton's stunning Palm House (1844–48), his Temperate House (1860–62, when it was the world's largest greenhouse), Waterlily House (1852), and the Princess of Wales Conservatory (1987). The newest exhibition, Evolution, is in the 1950s Australia House.

KENSINGTON PALACE & GARDENS

It gives King William III a human dimension that he suffered from asthma, a modern complaint, and so moved out of dank Whitehall Palace to a mansion in the clean air of tiny Kensington village. This royal home retains a domestic feel.

The perfect location The year he became king, 1689, William and his wife Mary bought their mansion, perfectly positioned for London socializing and country living. They brought in Sir Christopher Wren and Nicholas Hawksmoor to remodel and enlarge the house, and moved in for Christmas.

A favorite royal home Despite the small rooms, George I introduced palatial grandeur with Colen Campbell's staircase and state rooms, elegantly decorated by William Kent. Meanwhile, Queen Anne added the Orangery (the architect was Hawksmoor, the woodcarver Grinling Gibbons) and annexed a chunk of royal Hyde Park, a trick repeated by George II's wife, Queen Caroline, who created the Round Pond and Long Water to complete the 275-acre Kensington Gardens. Today, a wide variety of trees are the backdrop for sculptures by G. F. Watts, Henry Moore, and George Frampton, whose image of the fairytale Peter Pan is near the Long Water.

A very special childhood On May 24, 1819, Queen Victoria was born here. She was baptized in the splendid Cupola Room, spent her childhood in rooms overlooking the gardens (now filled with Victoria memorabilia) and, on June 20, 1837, learned she was to be queen. Moving into Buckingham Palace, she later fully opened to the public the State Apartments and gardens of her childhood home.

HIGHLIGHTS

- King's Grand Staircase
- Presence Chamber
- Wind dial in the King's Gallery
- King's Drawing Room
- Princess Victoria's dolls' house
- Round Pond
- Summer tea in the Orangery
- Walks
- Serpentine Gallery
- Italian Gardens

INFORMATION

- C6
- Kensington Gardens, W8
- 0171-937 9561
- Mon–Sat 9–5, Sun 11–5 (last admission 4:15). Closed Dec 24–26, Jan 1, Good Fri. Closed for major refurbishment Sep–May
- Café (£) in palace (winter) or Orangery (summer)
- High Street Kensington; Queensway
- Few
- Expensive; family tickets
- Victoria & Albert Museum (➤ 28); Science Museum (➤ 27); Natural History Museum (➤ 26)
- Guided tour every 30 mins

NATURAL HISTORY MUSEUM

HIGHLIGHTS

- Cromwell Road façade
- Giant gold nugget
- Fossilized frogs
- Lapis lazuli from Afghanistan
- How the memory works
- Prehistoric animals
- Marine Invertebrate Gallery

INFORMATION

- 🔲 C7
- ✉ Cromwell Road, SW7
- ☎ 0171-938 9123
- ◉ Mon–Sat 10–5:50, Sun 11–5:50. Closed Dec 23–26
- 🍴 Meals, snacks, picnic areas
- 🚇 South Kensington
- ♿ Excellent
- 💱 Expensive; free after 4:30 Mon–Fri, after 5 Sat, Sun
- ↔ Science (➤ 27) and Victoria & Albert museums (➤ 28), Kensington Palace (➤ 25)
- ❓ Regular tours; lectures, films, workshops

Top: diplodocus skeleton in the entrance hall
Below: the East Wing

This is one of my favorite museum buildings: it looks like a striped, Romanesque cathedral and is wittily decorated with a zoo of animals to match its contents: extant animals on the west side, extinct ones on the east side.

Two museums in one The Life Galleries of this family museum were originally part of the British Museum but overflowed and were housed in Alfred Waterhouse's honey-and-blue striped building in 1880. They tell the story of life on earth. The Earth Galleries tell the story of the earth itself, beginning with a 300-million-year-old fossil of a fern blowing in the wind.

Dinosaurs in the Life Galleries The nave of Waterhouse's cathedral contains a plaster cast of the vast skeleton of the 150-million-year-old diplodocus (the original is in Pittsburg, PA). In the surrounding bays are foretastes of discoveries to be made in the galleries: a pygmy chimpanzee skeleton, huge deer antlers 11,000 years old, and much more. The lively exhibition galleries, now mostly re-modeled, focus on the dinosaur world, the human body, mammals, birds, the marine world, and "creepy crawlies" (the 800,000 known species of insect are added to every year), all with plenty of slides, models, and hands-on games.

The Earth Galleries On ground level, through Waterhouse Way, this less obviously interesting collection is in fact a fascinating exploration of our planet. A spectacular redevelopment, opening in phases, will include a central atrium with escalators traveling to various exhibitions.

SCIENCE MUSEUM

Even though I am no scientist, I find it thrilling to understand at last how a plane flies, how Newton's reflecting telescope worked or how we receive satellite television. This is science made fun.

Industry and science This museum, once part of the Victoria & Albert Museum, opened in 1857. It comes closest to fulfilling Prince Albert's educational aims when he founded the South Kensington Museums after the Great Exhibition of 1851. Its full title is the National Museum of Science and Industry. Therefore, over the five floors, which contain more than 60 collections, the story of human industry, discovery and invention is recounted through various tools and products, from exquisite Georgian cabinets to printing presses, machine looms and, today, a satellite launcher.

Science made fun People walk, talk, laugh and get excited by what they see here. It is fun for all ages to see how things important to us every day were invented and then developed for use. The spinning wheel, steam-engine, car and television have changed our lives. The industrial society in which we live could not do without plastic, but how is it made?

All kinds of science The 70 or so galleries arranged over six floors vary from rooms of beautiful 18th-century objects to hands-on galleries and in-depth explanations of abstract concepts. This means you can use the hands-on equipment in Flight Lab to learn the basic principles of flying, and then use this knowledge in the Flight Gallery next door. The Wellcome Museum of the History of Medicine, on the topmost floors, includes an exhibit on prehistoric bone surgery and an X-ray room.

HIGHLIGHTS

- Demonstrations
- Taking part in Launch Pad
- The hands-on basement area
- Flight Lab
- Apollo 10 module
- Puffing Billy
- Amy Johnson's aeroplane, *Jason*
- 18th-century watches and clocks
- Health Matters
- Historical characters explaining their achievements

INFORMATION

- ✚ C7
- ✉ Exhibition Road, SW7
- ☎ 0171-938 8000
- ◷ Daily 10–6.
  Closed Dec 24–26
- 🍴 Café, picnic area
- Ⓠ South Kensington
- ♿ Excellent, plus helplines
  0171-938 9788
- ⊞ Expensive; family and season tickets, South Kensington Museums season ticket; free after 4:30 daily
- ❓ Guided tours; demonstrations, historic characters, lectures, films, workshops

Top: the Apollo 10 module in the Exploration of Space Gallery

VICTORIA & ALBERT MUSEUM

HIGHLIGHTS

- Medieval ivory carvings
- Jones porcelain collection
- Glass Gallery
- Shah Jahan's Jade Cup
- Canning Jewel
- Cartoons, Raphael
- Great Bed of Ware
- Frank Lloyd Wright Room

INFORMATION

- ✚ D7
- ✉ Cromwell Road, SW7
- ☎ 0171-938 8500
- ⊙ Mon noon–5:50, Tue–Sun 10–5:50. Closed Dec 24–26, Jan 1, Good Fri, May 1
- 🍴 Basement restaurant, café
- Ⓢ South Kensington
- ♿ Very good
- 🔲 "Voluntary" donation expensive; charge for special exhibitions
- ↔ Natural History Museum (➤ 26), Science Museum (➤ 27)
- ❓ Tours, talks, courses, concerts

Detail, façade

Part of the Victoria and Albert Museum's glory for me is that each room is unexpected; it may contain a French boudoir, plaster casts of classical sculptures or exquisite contemporary glass, diverting me so happily that sometimes I never reach my original goal.

An optimistic foundation The V&A, as it is fondly known, started as the South Kensington Museum. It was Prince Albert's vision: arts and science objects available to all people to inspire them to invent and create, with the accent on commercial design and craftsmanship. Since it opened in 1857, its collection has become so encyclopedic and international that it is today the world's largest decorative arts museum.

Bigger and bigger Its size is unmanageable: 145 galleries cover 7 miles of gallery space on six floors. Its content is even more so: barely 5 percent of the 44,000 objects in the Indian department can be on show. Larger museum objects include whole London house façades, grand rooms, and the Raphael Cartoons. Despite this, contemporary work has always been energetically bought, and continues to be: more than 2,000 works on paper are acquired annually, mostly new, and more than 60 percent of furniture entering the museum is 20th-century.

Riches and rags Not every V&A object is precious: there are everyday things, unique pieces and opportunities to discover a fascination for a new subject—perhaps lace, ironwork, tiles, Indian paintings, or Japanese textiles. The best way to tackle the V&A is either to select a favorite piece and go headlong for it, or wander happily for an hour or so, feasting on any objects that catch your eye.

KENWOOD HOUSE & HAMPSTEAD HEATH

As a north Londoner, I find sunny Sunday mornings on Hampstead Heath an essential part of my life: locals walk their dogs and babies, sit reading the newspapers, enjoy the fine London views, and drop into Kenwood House to see a Rembrandt or two.

Kenwood House When in 1754 William Murray, Earl of Mansfield and George III's Chief Justice, bought his country house outside pretty Hampstead village spa, he brought in London's most fashionable architect, Robert Adam, to remodel it, and employed Humphry Repton to landscape the gardens. A later owner, Edward Guinness, Earl of Iveagh, hung the walls with Rembrandts, Gainsboroughs, Vermeers and Romneys before giving the whole package, the Iveagh Bequest, to the nation.

The people's heath When Victorian London was expanding, it was the people of Hampstead who saved their valuable, open heathland from the developers' claws. Since 1829 they have preserved, piece by piece, a total of 825 acres of rolling woodland, open grass and spectacular views—the walled Hill Garden was added only in 1960. It is "to be kept forever ... open, unenclosed and unbuilt on."

A place of many moods The heath is full of action and color when weekend kite-flyers meet on Parliament Hill. It is a place for sports, perhaps swimming or boating in Hampstead Ponds, playing hockey on East Heath, enjoying a game of tennis, or simply taking a quiet walk. There are arts celebrations, too, the best of which are the summer lakeside concerts that Londoners listen to as they picnic on the sloping lawns in front of Kenwood House.

HIGHLIGHTS

- Azaleas in the Hill Garden
- Library in Kenwood House
- Lakeside concerts
- London view from beside Kenwood House
- Oak, beech, and sweet chestnut woods
- Parliament Hill
- Crossing the Heath from Hampstead to Highgate
- Rembrandt's *Portrait of the Artist* in Kenwood House
- Carpets of spring daffodils around Kenwood

INFORMATION

- ✉ Kenwood House, Hampstead Lane, NW3
- ☎ 0181-348 1286
- 🕐 Apr–Sep, daily 10–6; Oct–Mar, daily 10–4. Closed Dec 24–25. Park open daily 8AM–dusk
- 🍴 Restaurant, café
- Ⓔ Golders Green (for Kenwood); Hampstead, Belsize Park, Highgate, Kentish Town (for the Heath)
- 🚌 210, 271 (for Kenwood), 214, C2, C11, C12 (for Parliament Hill),
- 🚉 Gospel Oak, Hampstead Heath (North London Link)
- ♿ Good
- 💷 Free
- ❓ Guided tours for parties; indoor and outdoor concerts

7

REGENT'S PARK

HIGHLIGHTS

- Queen Mary's Gardens
- Lakeside strolls
- Lolling on deck chairs by the bandstand
- Nature Study Centre
- Boating on the lake
- Nesfield's restored Avenue Gardens
- Canal boat from the Zoo to Little Venice
- 98 species of duck
- Picnicking on the lake's north bank
- Summer barbecues and open-air theater

INFORMATION

- ➕ E3
- ✉ Marylebone Road, NW1
- ☎ 0171-486 7905
- ⏱ Whole park open by 7AM daily, until shortly before dusk (times vary monthly, posted on information boards at each gate)
- 🍴 Restaurant, cafés
- Ⓜ Baker Street, Regent's Park, Great Portland Street, Camden Town
- ♿ Very good
- ↔ London Zoo (➤31), Madame Tussaud's Waxworks (➤59), Planetarium (➤59)
- ❓ Information boards at each entrance include plans, boats for rent on lake and children's boating pond, weekend bandstand music. Open-Air Theatre stages theater and musicals May–Sep

Regent's Park contains all I could wish for: big open spaces, a lake to row on, spectacular gardens, ducks and swans in quantity, a variety of ideal picnic spots, theater and music and free peeks at the elephants in the zoo.

The Prince's plan Regent's Park is the result of a remarkable coincidence of royal enlightenment, architectural theater, peaceful times, and a large tract of land becoming available. In 1811 the Prince Regent, later George IV, and his architect John Nash conceived and completed a Regency backbone for London stretching from St. James's Park up Regent Street and Portland Place to Regent's Park. After vast earth-moving activities, the park was given its undulating lawns, lake, garden and trees, all encircled by grand terrace backdrops and dotted with just eight of the 56 planned villas.

From the nobles to the people What was designed as a garden city for nobles is now the most elegant of London parks. It has been open to the public since 1835, when Regent's Canal was the busiest stretch of canal in Britain. Londoners flocked there to visit the Zoo, Inner Circle (later Queen Mary's) Gardens, and Avenue Gardens, which W. A. Nesfield designed in 1864. Its 487 acres easily absorb Muslims strolling from the gold-domed Central Mosque, patrons of the Open-Air Theatre and cricketers—and there's still space to spare.

The canal at Little Venice

LONDON ZOO

When we go to the zoo we always spend time looking at the wonderful gentle Asian elephants—first from Regent's Park, then inside the zoo—having a bath, throwing dust over their backs, eating, lazing about looking contented and playing with their keeper.

Exotic animals for Londoners In 1826 Sir Stamford Raffles, who established Singapore Colony, founded the Zoological Society of London with Sir Humphry Davy. Four years later it opened five acres of its gardens to the public, with immediate success. The Society's own collection of exotic animals—zebras, monkeys, kangaroos and bears—was soon enlarged by the royal menagerie from Windsor and the royal zoo from the Tower of London.

Extraordinary animals The gardens were expanded to 36 acres; new residents included giraffes, whose arrival in 1836 set a trend for giraffe-patterned fabric. Jumbo and Alice, the African elephants, were also exceedingly popular. Meanwhile, the world's first reptile house, aquarium, and insect houses were constructed.

A modern zoo Aware of the controversy over zoos, London Zoo is maintaining its place at the forefront of animal conservation and education, housing the Institute of Zoology, which carries out research, and funding fieldwork. The new Children's Zoo has a "petting paddock" with farm animals, ponies, camels and llamas, and a center to teach children how to care for pets. Ming Ming the panda has returned from China, and elsewhere monkeys swing about, sloths hang from branches, penguins splash around, and the big cats roar.

HIGHLIGHTS

- Asian elephants
- Big cats
- Children's Zoo Pet Care Centre
- Lord Snowdon's aviaries
- Reversed lighting to see nocturnal mammals
- Feeding time for penguins
- Cavorting chimpanzees
- Polar bears
- Baby rhinos

INFORMATION

- ✚ E2 (for entrance)
- ✉ Regent's Park, NW1
- ☎ 0171-722 3333
- ◷ Apr–Oct, daily 10–5:30; Nov–Mar, daily 10–4. Closed Dec 25
- 🍴 Restaurant, cafés & kiosks
- Ⓔ Camden Town
- 🚉 Camden Town (Thameslink)
- ♿ Good
- 🔠 Very expensive
- ↔ Regent's Park (➤ 30)
- ❓ Lectures, talks, workshops, regular animal feeding times, animal action programs daily

Top: the elephant enclosure

BUCKINGHAM PALACE

HIGHLIGHTS

- Liveried beadles in the Queen's Gallery
- Changing of the Guard
- State Coach, Royal Mews
- Nash's façade, Quadrangle
- Gobelin tapestries in the Guard Room
- Throne Room
- Van Dyck's portrait of Charles I and family
- Table of Grand Commanders, Blue Drawing Room
- Secret royal door in the White Drawing Room
- Garden Shop

INFORMATION

- ✚ F6
- ✉ The Mall, SW1
- ☎ 0171-839 1377
- ◷ Queen's Gallery: Tue–Sat 10–6, Sun 2–5 (during exhibitions)
  Royal Mews: Apr–Sep, Tue–Thu 12–4; Oct–Mar, Wed 12–4. Closed Ascot week and ceremonial occasions
  Buckingham Palace: early Aug–late Sep, daily 9:30–5:30 (last entry 4:30)
- Ⓔ Victoria, St. James's Park, Green Park
- 🚇 Victoria (BR)
- ♿ Excellent
- ↔ Changing the Guard (➤ 22), St. James' Park (➤ 33)
- ❓ No photography but plenty of photographs to buy

Of the London houses now open to visitors, the Queen's own home where she spends much of the year must be the most fascinating of all: where else can you see a living sovereign's private art, drawing rooms, and horse harnesses.

Yet another palace The British sovereigns have moved around London quite a bit over the years: from Westminster to Whitehall to Kensington and St. James's, and finally to Buckingham Palace. It was George III who, in 1762, bought the prime-site mansion, Buckingham House, as a gift for his new bride, the 17-year-old Queen Charlotte, leaving St. James's Palace to be the official royal residence.

Grand improvements When the Prince Regent finally became King George IV in 1820, he and his architect, John Nash, made extravagant changes using honey-colored Bath stone, all to be covered up by Edward Blore's façade added for Queen Victoria. Today, the 600 rooms and 40-acre garden include the State Apartments, offices for the Royal Household, a movie theater, swimming pool and the Queen's private rooms overlooking Green Park.

Queen Elizabeth II opens her home The Queen inherited the world's finest private art collection and in 1962 built the Queen's Gallery so everyone could enjoy changing exhibitions selected from her riches. Nearby, in the Royal Mews, Nash's stables and storerooms house gleaming fairytale coaches, harnesses, and other apparel for royal ceremonies. Make sure you do not miss the Buckingham Palace Summer Opening, when visitors can wander through the grand State Rooms, resplendent with gold, pictures, porcelain, tapestries and, of course, thrones.

St. James's Park

Even if I drop in to St. James's Park merely to eat a sandwich and laze on a deck chair to listen to the band's music, on my way through I can usually spot a trio of palaces across the duck-filled lake and over the tips of the weeping willows.

Royal through and through St. James's Park is the oldest and most thoroughly royal of London's nine royal parks, surrounded by the Palace of Westminster, the remains of Whitehall Palace, St. James's Palace and Buckingham Palace. Kings and their courtiers have been frolicking here since Henry VIII laid out a deer park in 1532 and built a hunting lodge that became St. James's Palace. James I began the menagerie, which included pelicans, crocodiles, and an elephant who drank a daily gallon of wine.

French order Charles II, influenced by Versailles, near Paris, redesigned the park to include a canal (where he swam), Birdcage Walk (where he kept his aviaries) and the graveled Mall where he played pell mell, a courtly French game similar to croquet. Then George IV, helped by Nash and influenced by Humphry Repton, softened the garden's formal French lines into the English style, making this 93-acre park of blossoming shrubs and undulating, curving paths a favorite with all romantics.

Nature dominates As the park is an important migration point and breeding area for birds, two full-time ornithologists look after up to 1,000 birds from more than 45 species. Among the fig, plane and willow trees, seek out the pelicans living on Duck Island, a tradition begun when the Russian Ambassador gave some to Charles II.

HIGHLIGHTS

- Springtime daffodils
- Whitehall from the lake bridge
- Feeding the pelicans, 4PM
- Views to Buckingham Palace
- Duck Island in springtime
- The fact that it is still not enclosed

INFORMATION

- F6
- The Mall, SW1
- 0171-930 1793
- Daily dawn–midnight
- Restaurant, café
- St. James's Park, Green Park, Westminster
- Victoria
- Very good
- Free
- Buckingham Palace (➤ 32), Changing the Guard (➤ 22), Banqueting House (➤ 37)
- Occasional bird talks, summer bandstand music

The Whitehall skyline seen from the park

TATE GALLERY

HIGHLIGHTS

- Double portrait of the Cholmondeley Sisters
- *John, 10th Viscount Kilmorey*, Gainsborough
- *The Opening of Waterloo Bridge*, Constable
- *Interior at Petworth*, Turner
- *The Ball on Shipboard*, Tissot
- Roomful of red Rothkos
- *Reading Woman with Parasol*, Matisse
- *The Three Dancers*, Picasso
- *White Relief*, Ben Nicholson
- *The Kiss*, Rodin

INFORMATION

- G8
- Millbank, SW1
- 0171-887 8000
- Mon–Sat 10–5:50, Sun 2–5:50. Closed Dec 24–26, Jan 1, Good Fri, May Day Bank Holiday
- Restaurant, café
- Pimlico
- Victoria
- Very good
- Free; charge for special exhibitions
- Westminster Abbey (➤ 35)
- Guided tours; Tate Inform audioguide; lectures, workshops, films, Turner Study room

The annual Tate rehang by the director is a winter highlight: familiar pictures reappear in different places, and there are plenty of new works, both British and modern, to get to know.

Two for one The Tate, opened in 1897, is named after the sugar millionaire Henry Tate, who paid for the core building and donated his Victorian pictures to put inside it. Today it houses two large national collections, displaying some of each: British art from the 16th century to around 1900; and international modern art from the Impressionists until the present day. The annual rehangs emphasize different aspects of both collections.

British art In rooms to the left of the central halls (filled with sculptures) you may well find the large icon-like portrait of Elizabeth I by Nicholas Hilliard and the Tate's earliest dated picture, John Bette's *Man in a Black Cap* (1545). There are portraits by Van Dyck, Hogarth, Gainsborough, and Reynolds, illustrations by Blake, landscapes by Constable and, in Room 9, pictures by the Pre-Raphaelites. The Turner Collection is housed in the Clore Gallery, (through Room 18), designed by James Stirling.

Modern international art Across the central halls, you will enter the modern rooms, where the more controversial works generate plenty of noisy discussion. You may find works by Monet, Matisse and Picasso, or by the more recent Mark Rothko and Jasper Johns, or by the British artists David Hockney and Peter Blake. But space is limited. This collection is to move into Giles Gilbert Scott's splendid Bankside Power Station in the year 2000, and there are Tate outposts in Liverpool and at St. Ives in Cornwall.

WESTMINSTER ABBEY

It requires an effort to get there, but my favorite time in the Abbey is the 8AM service in tiny St. Faith's Chapel, and then wandering in the silent nave and cloisters before the noisy tours arrive.

The kernel of London's second city It was Edward the Confessor who in the 11th century began the rebuilding of the modest Benedictine abbey church of St. Peter which was consecrated in 1065. The first sovereign to be crowned there was William the Conqueror, on Christmas Day, 1066. Successive kings were patrons, as were the pilgrims who flocked to the Confessor's shrine. Henry III (1216–72) employed Master Henry de Reyns to re-begin the Gothic abbey that stands today, and Henry VII (1485–1509) built his Tudor chapel with its delicate fan-vaulting. Since William I, all sovereigns have been crowned here—even after Henry VIII broke with Rome in 1533 and made himself head of the Church of England; and all were buried here up to George II (after which Windsor became the royal burial place, ▶ 20–21).

The West Front

Daunting riches The Abbey is massive, full of monuments, and very popular. At the west door, enjoy the view and Master Henry's achievement, then look over the Victorian Gothic choir screen into Henry V's chantry. After seeing the chapels, the royal necropolis, and Poets' Corner, leave time for the peaceful Cloisters.

HIGHLIGHTS

- Portrait of Richard II
- Mid-morning choral singing
- Sir Isaac Newton memorial
- Thornhill's window
- Henry VII's Chapel
- Edward the Confessor's Chapel
- St. Faith's Chapel
- Tile floor, Chapter House
- Little Cloister and College Garden
- Weekday Sung Evensong (not Wed) at 5PM

INFORMATION

- ✚ G7
- ✉ Broad Sanctuary, SW1
- ☎ 0171-222 5152
- 🕐 Nave and Cloisters daily 8–6; Royal Chapels Mon–Fri 9:20–4:45, Sat 9:20–2:45, 3:45–6; Abbey open for amateur photography Wed 6PM–7:45PM (free). Abbey closed before special services; Royal Chapels closed Sun, Dec 24–28, Good Fri, Commonwealth Observance Day
- 🍴 Café in Cloisters
- Ⓜ Westminster
- 🚉 Victoria
- ♿ Good
- 💰 Free for services; Royal Chapels expensive
- ↔ Houses of Parliament (▶ 36)
- ❓ Guided tours

35

HOUSES OF PARLIAMENT

- View from Westminster Bridge
- Statue of Oliver Cromwell
- Big Ben
- Richard 1's equestrian statue
- Commons or Lords debates
- Line of Route Tours
- St. Stephen's Hall
- Westminster Hall
- State Opening of Parliament
- Jewel Tower

INFORMATION

- G7
- Westminster, SW1
- 0171-219 3000; 0171-219 4272 (Commons); 0171-219 3107 (Lords)
- Parliament: sits Mon, Tue, Thu 2:30; Wed 10, Fri 9:30. Closed Christmas, Easter, Whitsun (late May) and summer (late Jul – mid-Oct) recesses.
  Jewel Tower: daily 10–noon, 1–6 (closes 4, Nov 1–Mar 31). Closed Dec 24–26, Jan 1
- Westminster
- Waterloo
- Parliament: free; line up or apply for tickets from your embassy or consulate. Line of Route permits: Public Information Office, House of Commons, 1 Derby Gate. Jewel House: moderate
- Westminster Abbey (➤35)

Big Ben is for me the symbol of London; I love its tower, its huge clear clockface, its thundering hour bell whose name is now given to the whole tower, and the way it glows like a reassuring beacon when illuminated at night.

Powerhouse for Crown and State William the Conqueror made Westminster his seat of rule to watch over the London merchants (he also built the Tower of London, ➤48). It was soon the center of government for England, then Britain, then a globe-encircling empire. It was also the principal royal home until Henry VIII moved to Whitehall.

Mother of parliaments Here the foundations of Parliament were laid according to Edward I's Model Parliament of 1295: a combination of elected citizens, lords, and clergy. This developed into the House of Commons (elected Members of Parliament) and the House of Lords (unelected senior members of State and Church). Henry VIII's Reformation Parliament ended Church domination of Parliament and made the Commons more powerful than the Lords.

A building fit for an empire Having survived the Catholic conspiracy to blow up Parliament (on November 5, 1605, Guy Fawkes night), almost all the buildings were destroyed by a fire in 1834. Kingdom and empire needed a new headquarters. With Charles Barry's plans and A. W. Pugin's detailed design, a masterpiece of Victorian Gothic was created. Behind the river façade decorated with statues of rulers, the Lords is on the left and the Commons on the right. If Parliament is in session, there is a flag on Victoria Tower or, at night, a light on Big Ben.

BANQUETING HOUSE

It is chilling to imagine Charles I calmly walking across the park from St. James's Palace to be beheaded outside the glorious hall built by his father. The magnificent ceiling was painted for Charles by Peter Paul Rubens.

London's most magnificent room This, the only surviving room of Whitehall Palace, was London's first building to be coated in smooth, white Portland stone. Designed by Inigo Jones and built between 1619 and 1622, it marked the beginning of James I's dream to replace his sprawling Tudor palace with a 2,000-room Palladian masterpiece. Only this was built. Inside, the King hosted small parties in the crypt and presided over lavish court ceremonies upstairs.

The Rubens ceiling The stunning ceiling was commissioned by James's son, Charles I. Painted between 1634 and 1636 by Peter Paul Rubens, the leading baroque artist based in Antwerp, the panels celebrate James I, who was also James VI of Scotland. Nine allegorical paintings show the unification of Scotland and England and the joyous benefits of wise rule, for which Rubens was paid £3,000 and given a knighthood.

The demise of Whitehall Palace This royal palace has brought a fair share of bad luck to its occupants. Cardinal Thomas Wolsey lived so ostentatiously that he fell from Henry VIII's favor. Henry moved in, making it his and his successors' main London royal residence. It was here that Charles I was beheaded on January 30, 1649, that William III suffered from the dank river air, and that a fire in 1698 wiped out all but the Banqueting House.

HIGHLIGHTS

- Sculpted head of Charles I
- Weathercock put on the roof by James II
- Rubens ceiling
- Allegory of James I between Peace and Plenty
- Allegory of the birth and coronation of Charles I
- Night-time concerts
- Whitehall river terrace in Embankment Gardens
- Le Sueur's equestrian statue of Charles I (top of Whitehall)

INFORMATION

- ✚ G6
- ✉ Whitehall, SW1
- ☎ 0171-930 4179
- 🕐 Mon–Sat 10–5; last admission 4:30. Closed Dec 24–29, public holidays and for government functions
- 🚇 Westminster, Charing Cross, Embankment
- ♿ None
- 💷 Moderate
- 🔗 Cabinet War Rooms (➤ 50), St. James's Park (➤ 33), National Gallery (➤ 39)
- ❓ Occasional concerts

Inigo Jones's façade

15

NATIONAL PORTRAIT GALLERY

HIGHLIGHTS

- *Self-portrait with Barbara Hepworth*, Ben Nicholson
- Icon-like *Richard II*
- *Elizabeth I*, Marcus Gheeraerts the Younger
- *Samuel Pepys*, John Hayl
- *Queen Victoria*, Sir George Hayter
- *The Brontë Sisters*, Branwell Brontë
- *Isambard Kingdom Brunel*, John Callcott
- *Florence Nightingale*, William White
- *Captain Scott*, Herbert Ponting
- *Sir Peter Hall*, Tom Phillips

INFORMATION

- ✚ G5
- ✉ St. Martin's Place, WC2
- ☎ 0171-306 0055
- ⏰ Mon–Sat 10–6, Sun 12–6. Closed Dec 24–26, Jan 1, Good Fri, May Day Bank Holiday
- 🚇 Leicester Square, Charing Cross
- 🚉 Charing Cross (BR)
- ♿ Good
- 🎟 Free, except for special exhibitions
- ↔ National Gallery (➤ 39)
- ❓ Lectures, events

It is always fascinating to see what some-one famous looks like and how they chose to be painted—I would never have expected Francis Drake to be in red courtier's, rather than sailor's, clothes.

A British record Founded in 1856 to collect portraits of the Great and Good in British life, and so inspire others to greatness, this now huge collection is the world's most comprehensive of its kind. There are oil paintings, watercolors, caricatures, silhouettes, and photographs.

Start at the top The galleries are arranged in chronological order, starting on the top floor (which can be reached by stairs or elevator). Henry VIII and some of his wives kick off a visual Who's Who of British history that moves through inventors, merchants, engineers, explorers, and empire builders to modern politicians, always accompanied by their observers, the writers. Brunel and Jenner are here, so too are Clive and Hastings, Winston Churchill, and Margaret Thatcher. There is Chaucer in his floppy hat, Kipling at his desk, and A. A. Milne with Christopher Robin and Winnie-the-Pooh on his knee. Some of the lesser-known sitters merit a close look, such as the 18th-century group portrait of the remarkable and extensive Sharp Family, who formed an orchestra and played at Fulham every Sunday.

A modern record, too At first, the Victorians insisted upon entry only after death, but this rule has been broken. Among the many contemporary portraits you may find those of the Princess Royal, Beatle Paul McCartney, fashion designer Zandra Rhodes, soccer player Bobby Charlton, and artist Peter Blake.

NATIONAL GALLERY

The façades may be unexciting, but here is a collection of tip-top pictures—and for free, so I can drop in for a few minutes' peace in front of Leonardo da Vinci's cartoon in the Sainsbury Wing or Rubens's ravishing 'Samson and Delilah'.

A quality collection Founded in 1824 with just 38 pictures, the National Gallery now has about 2,000 paintings, all on show. Spread throughout William Wilkins's neo-classical building and the new Sainsbury Wing extension, they provide an uncramped, extremely high-quality, concise panorama of European painting from Giotto to Cézanne. Most modern and British pictures are at the Tate Gallery (➤ 34).

Not royal, not only British Unusually for a national painting collection, the nucleus is not royal but the collection of John Julius Angerstein, a self-made financier. From the start it was open to all, including children, free of charge, and provided a wide spectrum of British painting, within a European context—aims that are still maintained.

A first visit To take advantage of the rich artistic panorama in this comparatively small gallery, select a room from each of the four chronologically arranged sections. Early pictures by Duccio di Buoninsegna, Jan van Eyck, Piero della Francesca and others fill the Sainsbury Wing. In the old building, 16th-century pictures, including Michelangelo's *Entombment*, are in the West Wing, while the North Wing is devoted to 17th-century artists such as Van Dyck, Rubens, Rembrandt, Velàzquez, and painters of the Dutch school. Finally, the East Wing runs from Chardin through Gainsborough to Monet, Matisse, and Picasso.

HIGHLIGHTS

- *Cartoon*, Leonardo da Vinci
- *Julius II*, Raphael Pope
- *The Arnolfini Wedding*, Van Eyck
- Equestrian portrait of Charles I by Van Dyck
- *The Triumph of Pan*, Poussin
- *Le Chapeau de Paille*, Rubens
- *The House of Cards*, Chardin
- *Mr. and Mrs. William Hallett*, Gainsborough
- *Bathers*, Cézanne
- View from Wilkins's entrance

INFORMATION

- ✚ G6
- ✉ Trafalgar Square, WC2
- ☎ 0171-839 3321
- 🕐 Mon–Sat 10–6, Sun 2–6. Closed Dec 24–26, Jan 1, Good Fri
- 🍴 Brasserie, basement café
- 🚇 Charing Cross, Leicester Square
- 🚆 Charing Cross (BR)
- ♿ Excellent
- 🎟 Free; charge for special exhibition
- ↔ National Portrait Gallery (➤ 38), St. James's Park (➤ 33)
- ❓ Guided tours; lectures, films, picture identification service, occasional and summer late Wed openings, till 8PM

COVENT GARDEN PIAZZA

HIGHLIGHTS

- Bedford arms and motto over the Market entrances
- St. Paul's Covent Garden
- 1920s and '30s Underground posters
- Craft stalls in Apple Market
- Cabaret Mechanical Museum
- Jubilee Hall Market
- How the Underground works, London Transport Museum
- Charles H. Fox's make-up shop, Tavistock Street
- Neal Street, nearby

INFORMATION

➕ G5
✉ Covent Garden Piazza, WC2
🍴 Plentiful, all prices
Ⓜ Covent Garden
🚆 Charing Cross
♿ Good
🎫 Free, except museums
↔ National Portrait Gallery (➤ 38), British Museum (➤ 43), Courtauld Institute Galleries (➤ 41), Dr. Johnson's House (➤ 52)

London Transport Museum

✉ 39 Wellington Street, WC2
☎ 0171-379 6344
🕐 Daily 10–6, last admission 5:15. Closed Dec 24–26
🍴 Café
♿ Very good
🎫 Expensive
❓ Weekend guided tours; lectures, films, workshops

It is always fun to cut through the Piazza, to see perhaps a family of clowns cavorting in front of St. Paul's Church, a busker cheering on the stall-holders, and people meeting up to enjoy the City.

London's first square Charles I was against expanding beyond the City but Francis Russell, the Earl of Bedford, owned a prime piece of land just west of it. Around 1630 the Earl paid the King £2,000 for a building license and used Inigo Jones to lay out London's first residential square. An instant success, it became a distinctive London feature.

Covent Garden When society left, the vegetable market moved in, together with taverns, gambling dens and prostitutes. Charles Fowler's Central Market (1831) brought order, as did Floral, Flower, and Jubilee Halls, making this London's central fruit and vegetable

A Punch & Judy show

market until 1974. Locals saved the area from demolition, and today the restored halls and spruced up streets make the Piazza London's most convivial meeting place.

London Transport Museum This tells the story of the world's largest urban public transportation system, which covers more than half a million miles. There are buttons to push, and plenty of vehicles. Star attractions include the Underground simulator, the touch screens in six languages, actors on the vehicles—and the shop.

COURTAULD INSTITUTE GALLERIES

These sumptuously decorated galleries hung with Impressionist paintings—Renoir's **La Loge**, *Manet's* **Bar at the Folies-Bergères**, *Cézannes, Gauguins and many more—are for me the perfect antidote to a gray, cloud-coated London day.*

One man's vision The industrialist Samuel Courtauld began collecting French Impressionist and Post-Impressionist paintings in 1921. Ten years later he founded the Courtauld Institute of Art. Using his own mansion designed by Robert Adam in Portman Square, he hoped that art history students would learn about paintings in the setting of fine architecture and furniture. In its new home, the Courtauld fulfills his aim perfectly.

A palatial home A majestic, triple-arched gateway leads into Sir William Chambers's rather dull English Palladian government offices (1776–86) —no match for th work of his contemporary fellow Scot, the highly fashionable Robert Adam. Before the Embankment was built, its river façade met the Thames with great basement arches and a watergate, which you can see from Waterloo Bridge. The 11 galleries fill a string of lavishly decorated, restored rooms, once the home of the Royal Academy (➤ 51).

Six collections in one After Courtauld, five other collectors donated their art. Lord Lee of Fareham presented Old Masters and British works; art critic Roger Fry gave his collection; Sir Robert Witt gave his drawings (now the Witt Library, which fills the vaults); the Mark Gambier-Parry Bequest includes Italian Renaissance panels; and Count Antoine Seilern's Prince Gate Collection includes baroque painters such as Rubens, Tiepolo, and Van Dyck.

HIGHLIGHTS

- *Card Players*, Cézanne
- *Nevermore*, Gauguin
- *Peach Trees in Blossom*, van Gogh
- *Bar at the Folies Bergère*, Manet
- *La Lodge*, Renoir
- Any of 32 Rubens paintings
- Beechey's portrait of Queen Charlotte
- *Entombment*, Master of Flemalle
- River façade viewed from Waterloo Bridge

INFORMATION

- ✚ G5
- ✉ Somerset House, Strand, WC2
- ☎ 0171-873 2526
- Mon–Sat 10–6, Sun 2–6 (last admission 5:15). Closed Dec 24–26
- 🍴 Café
- 🎭 Temple
- 🚇 Blackfriars (BR, Thameslink), Charing Cross (BR)
- ♿ Excellent
- 🔉 Moderate
- ↔ Covent Garden (➤ 40), Dr. Johnson's House (➤ 50), Sir John Soane's Museum (➤ 42)
- ❓ Guided tours (pre-arranged); talks by Institute students, summer concerts, prints and drawings study room

Top: detail, Gauguin's
Nevermore

41

19

SIR JOHN SOANE'S MUSEUM

HIGHLIGHTS

- *The Rake's Progress, The Election, Hogarth*
- Sarcophagus of Seti I
- Lawrence's portrait of Soane
- Monk's Parlour
- Works by Turner, Canaletto
- Model Room

INFORMATION

- ✚ G5
- ✉ 13 Lincoln's Inn Field,s WC2
- ☎ 0171-405 2107
- 🕐 Tue–Sat 10–5, 1st Tue of month 6–9.
  Closed Dec 24–26, Jan 1, Good Fri
- Ⓗ Holborn
- 🚇 Farringdon
- ♿ Free
- ↔ British Museum (➤ 43), Courtauld Institute Galleries (➤ 41), Dickens House (➤ 44)
- ❓ Guided tours Sat 2:30

As I move about the gloriously over-furnished rooms of Soane's two houses—he outgrew one so built a second next door—and into the calm upstairs drawing-room, his presence is so strong that I would not be surprised if he was there to greet me.

Soane the architect This double treasure-house in leafy Lincoln's Inn Fields, Central London's largest square, is where the neo-classical architect Sir John Soane lived. First he designed no. 12 and lived there from 1792. Then, outgrowing this, he bought no. 13 next door, rebuilt it with cunningly proportioned rooms, and lived there from 1813 until his death in 1837. Meanwhile, he also designed such landmark buildings as Holy Trinity, on Marylebone Road (1824–28), and parts of the Treasury, Whitehall. His model for his masterpiece, the Bank of England, is here, testament to its scandalous destruction (re-created rooms now form the bank's museum, ➤ 50).

Soane the collector Soane was an avid collector. For him, every art object could inspire his work, so his rooms were a visual reference library. Hogarth's paintings unfold from the walls in layers. There are so many sculptures, paintings, and antiquities that unless you keep your eyes peeled you will miss a Watteau drawing, a Greek vase, or something even better.

The ghost of Soane Sir John's ingenious designs pervade every room, as do the stories of his passion for collecting. For example, when an Egyptian sarcophagus arrived, he gave a three-day party in its honor.

Behind the façade a labyrinth of rooms houses a bizarre collection

BRITISH MUSEUM

I often play a game in the British Museum to choose my seven wonders of the world, and although the bronzes from the Indian Chola dynasty and the lion-filled reliefs that once lined an Assyrian palace are always on my list, the others vary.

The physician founder Sir Hans Sloane, after whom Sloane Square is named, was a fashionable London physician, "interested in the whole of human knowledge" and an avid collector of everything from plants to prints. When he died in 1753 aged 92 he left his collection of more than 80,000 objects to the nation on condition that it was given a permanent home. Thus began the British Museum, opened in 1759 in a 17th-century mansion, Britain's first public museum and now its largest, covering 13½ acres.

It grew and it grew To Sloane's collection were added many others. Kings George II, III, and IV made magnificent gifts, as did others. These, with the Townley and Elgin Marbles, burst the building's seams and the architect Robert Smirke was commissioned to build a grand new museum, completed by his son, Sydney, in 1857. Even so, because the booty from expeditions and excavations poured in continuously, the Natural History collections went to South Kensington (►26), and ethnography to the Museum of Mankind (►51).

Coming to grips with the British Museum A good way to explore "that old curiosity shop in Great Russell Street" is to use the main entrance, pick up a plan, see what special events are on, choose at the most three rooms to see and set off to find them. For peace and quiet, it is worth going early.

HIGHLIGHTS

- Oriental antiquities
- The clocks, which all chime on the hour
- Rosetta Stone
- Current prints and drawings
- Islamic Art
- Mildenhall and Sutton Hoo treasures
- Elgin Marbles
- Assyrian and Egyptian rooms
- Lindisfarne Gospels
- 295-ft-long King's Library

INFORMATION

- ✚ G4
- ✉ Great Russell Street, WC1
- ☎ 0171-636 1555
- ◷ Mon–Sat 10–5, Sun 2:30–6, 1st Tue each month 6–9pm. Closed Dec 24–26, Jan 1, Good Fri, May Day Bank Holiday
- 🍽 Restaurant, café
- Ⓖ Holborn, Tottenham Court Road
- ♿ Very good
- Free; charge for some temporary exhibitions, tours and late opening
- ↔ Percival David Foundation of Chinese Art (►51), Covent Garden Piazza (►40)
- ❓ Gallery talks; guided tours; second entrance in Montague Place, lectures

21

DICKENS HOUSE

INFORMATION

- H4
- 48 Doughty Street, WC1
- 0171-405 2127
- Mon–Sat 10–5. Closed Dec 25 –Jan 4 and some public holidays
- Russell Square, Chancery Lane, King's Cross
- King's Cross
- Few
- Moderate
- British Museum (➤43), Percival David Foundation of Chinese Art (➤50–1), Sir John Soane's Museum (➤42)
- Information on regular Dickens walks

Standing beside Dickens's desk and chair in the house where he and his young wife lived, it is easy to imagine him going off on his long London walks to research deprived Victorian life while he was writing 'Oliver Twist'.

Dickens's London homes Of Charles Dickens's many London homes, this is the only survivor. He lived here between 1837 and 1839, moving from Furnival's Inn, Holborn, after he got married, and leaving when his growing family forced him to go to a larger house in Devonshire Terrace. Forty-eight Doughty Street is part of a typical brick, flat-fronted, Regency terrace, but it is set in a particularly wide and handsome avenue that, like the nearby Bloomsbury Square, would have had gates at either end manned by liveried porters, and mewslanes for servants and deliveries.

Dickens at Doughty Street Here Dickens completed *Pickwick Papers*, wrote *Oliver Twist* and *Nicholas Nickleby*, and began *Barnaby Rudge*. Here, too, Dickens emerged from his pseudonym of "Boz" into the literary limelight—there are some marked-up prompt copies for his legendary literary readings. Other Dickens memorabilia includes a Fagin Toby-jug.

The Dickens Fellowship This society, which bought the house in 1924 and restored the drawing room to its original decor, cares for the world's most comprehensive Dickens library and many Dickens-related portraits, letters, and manuscripts. Do not miss Harlot Knight Brown's "Phiz" illustrations. If you want to get to know more about Dickens, visit the house and then join a guided walk to explore a bit of his London.

ST. PAUL'S CATHEDRAL

To sneak into St. Paul's for afternoon evensong and sit gazing up at the mosaics as the choir's voices soar, is to savor a moment of absolute peace and beauty.

Wren's London After the restoration of the monarchy in 1660, artistic patronage bloomed under Charles II. Then, when the Great Fire of London destroyed four-fifths of the City in 1666, Christopher Wren took center stage, being appointed King's Surveyor-General in 1669, aged just 37. The spires, towers and steeples of his 51 new churches (23 still stand) surrounded his masterpiece, St. Paul's.

The fifth St Paul's This cathedral church for the diocese of London was founded in A.D. 604 by King Ethelbert of Kent. The first four churches burned down. Wren's, built in stone and paid for with a special coal tax, was the first English cathedral built by a single architect, the only one with a dome, and the only one in the English baroque style. The funerals of Admiral Lord Nelson, the Duke of Wellington, and Sir Winston Churchill were held here; statues and memorials of Britain's famous crowd the interior and crypt.

The great climb The 530 steps to the top are worth the effort. Shallow steps rise to

the Whispering Gallery for good views of Thornhill's dome frescoes and Richmond and Salviati's Victorian mosaics. The external Stone Gallery has telescopes and benches; above is the Golden Gallery. Go early or late to avoid crowds.

HIGHLIGHTS

- Sung Evensong
- Frescoes and mosaics
- Wren's Great Model in the triforium (upstairs)
- Triple-layered dome, weighing 76,000 tons
- Jean Tijou's sanctuary gates
- Wellington's memorial
- *Light of the World*, Holman Hunt
- The great climb
- Wren's epitaph under the dome

INFORMATION

- ✚ J5
- ✉ St. Paul's Churchyard, EC4
- ☎ 0171-248 2705/236 4128
- 🕐 Mon–Sat 8:30–4. Galleries Mon–Sat 10–4:15. Services Mon–Sat 5, Sun 11, 3:15
- Ⓜ St. Paul's, Mansion House
- 🚉 City Thameslink, Cannon Street (BR)
- ♿ Very good
- 🅿 Moderate. Galleries: extra fee
- ↔ Museum of London (➤ 47), St. Margaret's Lothbury (➤ 55), Bank of England Museum (➤ 50), Dr. Johnson's House (➤ 52)
- ❓ Guided tours Mon–Sat 11, 11:30, 1:30, 2; bell-ringing practice some Tue, lunchtime organ recitals most Fri lunchtimes and some Thu evenings; July summer masses; prayers every hour on the hour

23

ST. BARTHOLOMEW-THE-GREAT

HIGHLIGHTS

- Rahere's tomb
- Richard Rich's tomb
- William Bolton's window
- Medieval font
- Tudor memorial to Sir Walter Mildmay
- Ramsden church silver
- Any choral service
- The two church cats, Matins and Evensong

INFORMATION

- ✠ J4
- ✉ West Smithfield, EC1
- ☎ 0171-606 5171 (8:30–4:30)
- 🕐 Mon–Fri 8:30– 4:30, Sat 10–3, Sun 2–6
  Sun services: 9AM, 11AM (choral), 6:30PM (choral)
- 🚇 Barbican, Farringdon, St. Paul's
- 🚉 Farringdon
- ♿ Good
- 💲 Free (donation encouraged)
- ↔ Museum of London (➤47), St. Paul's Cathedral (➤45)
- ❓ Exceptional choir

A Sunday evening spent at St. Bartholomew's is truly memorable: while trucks arrive at Smithfield's meat market, we answer the ringing bells and pass under the great stone arch into a hidden, medieval world for beautifully sung evensong.

A court jester for founder Henry I's court jester, Rahere, became an Augustinian canon. While on pilgrimage to Rome he was cured of malaria, had a vision of St. Bartholomew and took a vow. On his return, the King gave him land to found St. Bartholomew's Hospital and Priory— London's first hospital but one of four monasteries in the area.

London's oldest church Rahere's priory church, built in 1123, is London's oldest church, the City's only 12th-century monastic church and its best surviving piece of large-scale Romanesque architecture. The remains—the nave and cloisters are gone—give an idea of the magnificence of London's dozen or so medieval monastic churches.

Entering a different world The church lies through a 13th-century stone arch topped by a Tudor gatehouse, which once led into the great priory church's west end. Today, a path runs the length of what was the ten-bay nave down to the present west door. Here is the choir, the ambulatory, and the Lady Chapel (built by Rahere), whose roofs are supported by honey-colored walls and sturdy, circular columns. The minimal decoration makes the impact all the more powerful. Two tombs to two men sit uneasily together here: the founder, Rahere (died 1143, tomb 1404) and the destroyer, Richard Rich, who bought the building from Henry VIII after the dissolution of the monasteries.

MUSEUM OF LONDON

A visit here is easily the best way to cruise through London's 2,000 years of history, pausing to see a Roman shoe, the Lord Mayor's State Coach, or an old shop counter; and it is even built on top of the West Gate of London's Roman fort.

A museum for London This is the world's largest and most comprehensive city museum, opened in 1975 in a building by Powell and Moya. The collection combines the old Guildhall Museum's City antiquities with the London Museum's costumes and other culturally related objects. Plenty of building work and redevelopment in the City of London in the 1980s, allied with increased awareness about conservation, has ensured a steady flow of archeological finds into the collection.

A museum about London The story of London is long and can be confusing. The building is, appropriately, in the barbican of the Roman fort, and the rooms are laid out chronologically to keep the story clear. Starting with prehistoric and Roman times (do not miss the peep-hole window down to 2nd-century barbican remains), the rooms work through the medieval, Tudor and Stuart periods, where a highlight is the re-enactment of the Great Fire of London in 1666. The Georgian, Victorian, and 20th-century rooms mix low life with high, ranging from Newgate Gaol and the Blitz Experience to Spitalfields silks, empire grandeur, and high-fashion stores.

A museum about Londoners People make a city, so in every room it is Londoners who are really telling the story, whether it is through their Roman storage jars, their Tudor leather clothes, or their Suffragette posters.

HIGHLIGHTS

- Neolithic bowl
- Roman letter addressed "Londinio"
- Roman wall remnants
- Viking grave
- Fragments from the Eleanor Cross
- Tudor jewelry
- Model of Tudor London
- Pepys's chess set
- 15th-century paneled room
- World War II Gallery

INFORMATION

- ✚ J4
- ✉ 150 London Wall, EC2
- ☎ 0171-600 3699
- 🕐 Tue–Sat 10–5:50, Sun 12–5:50. Closed Dec 24–26, Jan 1
- 🍴 Restaurant, café
- Ⓜ Barbican, Moorgate, St. Paul's
- 🚆 Moorgate, Farringdon, Liverpool St., City Thameslink
- ♿ Excellent
- 💷 Moderate; all tickets valid for three months
- ↔ Barbican (► 78–79), St. Bartholomew-the-Great (► 46), St. Paul's Cathedral (► 45)
- ❓ Lectures, gallery talks and performances, seminars, workshops, "Made in London" film series

Mural depicting a scene from the Great Fire 47

25

H.M. THE TOWER OF LONDON

HIGHLIGHTS

- Medieval Palace
- Raleigh's room
- Imperial State Crown
- Tower ravens
- Grand Punch Bowl, 1829
- St. John's Chapel

INFORMATION

- ✚ K5
- ☎ 0171-709 0765
- 🕐 Mon–Sat 9–6, Sun 10–6 (Nov–Feb till 5). Closed Dec 24–26, Jan 1
- 🚇 Tower Hill
- 🚉 Fenchurch Street, Cannon Street, London Bridge
- ♿ Excellent for Jewel House
- 💰 Very expensive
- ↔ Tower Bridge Museum (➤ 57), Design Museum (➤ 50), H.M.S. *Belfast* (➤ 57)
- ❓ Tours every 30 mins

Yeoman Warders or "Beefeaters" have guarded the Tower since 1485

The newly restored medieval palace, where Edward I lived at the end of the 12th century, brings the Tower alive as the royal palace and place of pageantry it was; for me, it's more interesting than the Crown Jewels.

Medieval fortress The Tower of London is Britain's best medieval fortress. William the Conqueror (1066–87) began it as a show of brute force, and Edward I (1272–1307) completed it. William's Caen stone White Tower, built within old Roman walls, was an excellent defense: it was 90 feet high, with walls 15 feet thick and space for soldiers, servants and nobles. Henry III began the Inner Wall, the moat, his own watergate—and the royal zoo. Edward I completed the Inner Wall, built the Outer Wall, several towers, and Traitor's gate, and moved the mint and crown jewels here from Westminster.

Scenes of splendor and horror Stephen (1135–54) was the first king to live here; James I (1603–25) the last. From here Edward I went into procession to his coronation and Henry VIII paraded through the City bedecked in cloth of gold. Here the Barons seized the Tower to force King John to put his seal to the Magna Carta in 1215; and here two princes were murdered while their uncle was being crowned Richard III.

Seven centuries of history The Tower has been palace, fortress, state prison and execution site. There is much to see. Come early and see the Crown Jewels before the lines grow. You can always use a re-entry permit to take a break along the Wharf.

LONDON's
best

MUSEUMS & GALLERIES

Dulwich Picture Gallery

Dulwich Picture Gallery's magnificent core collection of 400 paintings was assembled for the King of Poland's projected national gallery. When the king abdicated, it was offered unsuccessfully to Britain for the same purpose. The art dealer who put it together, Noel Desenfans, gave it to Sir Francis Bourgeois, who donated it to Dulwich College. Opened in 1814, it was England's first public art gallery.

BANK OF ENGLAND MUSEUM

See how Britain's monetary system and banking ideas have grown since 1694.

➕ J5 ✉ Bartholomew Lane, EC3 ☎ 0171-601 5545 🕐 Mon–Fri 10–5. Closed Dec 25–26, Bank holiday 🚇 Bank 🎫 Free

CABINET WAR ROOMS

The underground headquarters for Sir Winston Churchill's War Cabinet during World War II.

➕ G6 ✉ Clive Steps, King Charles Street, SW1 ☎ 0171-930 6961 🕐 Daily 9:30–5:15. Closed Dec 24–26 🚇 St James's Park, Westminster 🎫 Moderate

DESIGN MUSEUM

Founded by design guru Sir Terence Conran to stimulate design awareness; good shop.

➕ L6 ✉ Butler's Wharf, Shad Thames, SE1 ☎ 0171-403 6933 🕐 Mon–Fri 11:30–6; Sat, Sun 12–6. Closed Dec 25–26, Jan 1 🍴 Café 🚇 Tower Hill, London Bridge 🚊 London Bridge 🎫 Expensive

The Edwardian Room, in the Geffrye Museum

DULWICH PICTURE GALLERY

See panel.

➕ off map to southeast ✉ College Road, SE21 ☎ 0181-693 5254 🕐 Tue–Fri 10–5, Sat 11–5, Sun 2–5. Closed Dec 25–26, Bank holiday. 🍴 Summer tea tent 🚇 North or West Dulwich 🎫 Moderate; free on Fri

GEFFRYE MUSEUM

Almshouses furnished in period style, 1550–1950.

➕ K3 ✉ Kingsland Road, E2

☎ 0171-739 9893 🕙 Tue–Sat 10–5, Sun and Bank holiday Mon 2–5pm. Closed Dec 25–26, Jan 1, Good Fri 🍴 Café 🚇 Old Street then bus 22A, 243; Liverpool Street then bus 22B, 149 🎫 Free

HAYWARD GALLERY
Major venue for art exhibitions.
➕ H6 ✉ South Bank, SE1 ☎ 0171-416 5000 🕙 Daily 10–6 Closed Dec 24–26 🍴 Restaurant, café 🚇 Lambeth North, Elephant & Castle, Waterloo 🚉 Waterloo 🎫 Moderate

HOUSE MUSEUMS ►52

IMPERIAL WAR MUSEUM
Focuses on the social impact of 20th-century warfare through film, painting, and sound archives.
➕ H7 ✉ Lambeth Road, SE1 ☎ 0171-416 5000 🕙 Daily 10–6. Closed Dec 25–26, Jan 1 🍴 Restaurant, café 🚇 Lambeth North, Elephant & Castle, Waterloo 🚉 Waterloo 🎫 Moderate

MUSEUM OF MANKIND
The British Museum's Ethnography Department, full of masks, costumes, and musical instruments from non-Westernized societies.
➕ F5 ✉ 6, Burlington Gardens W1 ☎ 0171-323 8043 🕙 Mon–Sat 10–5, Sun 2:30–6. Closed Dec 25–26, Jan 1, Good Fri, May Bank holidays 🍴 Restaurant, café 🚇 Piccadilly 🎫 Free

A tableau in the Musuem of Mankind

MUSEUM OF THE MOVING IMAGE
The story of film, TV, and animation. Plenty of participation.
➕ H6 ✉ South Bank, SE1 ☎ 0171-928 3535 🕙 Daily 10–6, (last admission 5PM). Closed Dec 25–26 🚇 Embankment, Waterloo 🚉 Waterloo 🎫 Expensive

PERCIVAL DAVID FOUNDATION OF CHINESE ART
Sublime Chinese ceramics.
➕ G4 ✉ 53 Gordon Square, WC1 ☎ 0171-387 3909 🕙 Mon–Fri 10:30–5. Closed Dec 22–Jan 3, Easter, Bank holidays 🚇 Russell Square 🎫 Free

ROYAL ACADEMY
Major international art shows, plus the annual Summer Exhibition.
➕ F6 ✉ Burlington House, Piccadilly, W1 ☎ 0171-439 7438 🕙 Daily 10–6. Closed Dec 25–26, Good Fri 🍴 Restaurant, café 🚇 Green Park, Piccadilly 🎫 Expensive

TOWER BRIDGE MUSEUM ►57

WALLACE COLLECTION
See panel.
➕ E5 ✉ Hertford House, Manchester Square, W1 ☎ 0171 935 0687 🕙 Mon–Sat 10–5, Sun 2–5. Closed Dec 25–26, Jan 1, May Bank Holiday 🚇 Bond Street 🎫 Free

WHITECHAPEL ART GALLERY
Good art in the East End.
➕ L5 ✉ 80 Whitechapel High Street, E1 ☎ 0171-522 7888 🕙 Tue–Sat 11–5 (Wed till 8) 🍴 Café 🚇 Aldgate East 🎫 Free

The Wallace Collection

The Wallace Collection is the product of five generations of discerning art collectors. The 1st Marquess of Hertford bought Ramsays and Canalettos; the 2nd acquired Gainsborough's *Mrs. Robinson*; the 3rd preferred Sèvres and Dutch 17th-century pictures; and the 4th, in Paris during the Revolution, snapped up quality French art. His illegitimate son, Sir Richard Wallace, added his own Italian majolica, Renaissance armor, bronzes, and gold.

51

HOUSE MUSEUMS

Dr. Johnson's House

APSLEY HOUSE (WELLINGTON MUSEUM)
Splendid mansion built for Arthur Wellesley, the
Duke of Wellington (1759–1852).
✚ E6 ✉ Hyde Park Corner, SW1 ☎ 0171-499 5676 ⏰ Tue–Sun
11–5. Closed Dec 25–26, Jan 1, May Bank Holiday 🚇 Hyde Park
Corner 🎫 Expensive

CARLYLE'S HOUSE
Thomas Carlyle, Scottish philosopher and historian,
lived here from 1834 until his death in 1881.
✚ D8 ✉ 24 Cheyne Row, SW3 ☎ 0171-352 7087 ⏰ Apr–Oct,
Wed–Sun and Bank holiday Mon 11–4:30. Closed Nov–Mar 🚇 Sloane
Square 🎫 Moderate

CHISWICK HOUSE
Lord Burlington's exquisite country villa (1725–29).
✚ off map to southwest ✉ Burlington Lane, W4 ☎ 0181-995 0508
⏰ Apr–Sept, daily 10–1, 2–6; Oct–Mar, Wed–Sun 10–1, 2–4. Closed
Dec 24–26 🍴 Café 🚇 Turnham Green 🚉 Chiswick 🎫 Moderate

DR. JOHNSON'S HOUSE
Dr. Samuel Johnson lived here between 1749 and
1759 while compiling his dictionary.
✚ H5 ✉ 17 Gough Square EC4 ☎ 0171-353 3745
⏰ Mon–Sat 11–5:30; Oct–Apr closes 5. Closed Dec 25–26, Jan 1
🚇 Chancery Lane, Blackfriars 🚉 Blackfriars 🎫 Moderate

HAM HOUSE
Thameside mansion (1610), refurbished in baroque
style; 17th-century garden.
✚ off map to southwest ✉ Ham, Richmond, Surrey ☎ 0181-940
1950 ⏰ House Apr–Oct, Mon–Wed 1–5, Sat 1–5:30, Sun
11:30–5:30; Nov–Dec, Sat, Sun 1–4. Closed mid-Dec–Apr 1. Gardens:
Sat–Thu 10:30–6 (or dusk). Closed Dec 24–26 🍴 Restaurant
🚇 Richmond then bus 371 🎫 Expensive

LEIGHTON HOUSE
See panel.
✚ B7 ✉ 12 Holland Park Road, W14 ☎ 0171-602 3316
⏰ Mon–Sat 11–5:30. Closed Dec 24–26, Jan 1, Easter, Bank holiday
🚇 High Street Kensington 🎫 Free

SUTTON HOUSE ►60

WALLACE COLLECTION ►51

Leighton House
Lord Leighton made his reputa-
tion when Queen Victoria bought
one of his paintings. George
Aitchison then designed his home-
cum-studio (1861–66). The fashionable painter and esthete gave
the rooms rich red walls edged
with ebonized wood. Their center-
piece is the Arab Hall, one of
London's most exotic rooms, lined
with Leighton's Persian and
Saracenic blue and green tiles
collected during his travels.

STATUES & MONUMENTS

BURGHERS OF CALAIS
Auguste Rodin's muscular bronze citizens (1915).
✚ G7 ✉ Victoria Tower Gardens, SW1 🚇 Westminster

CHARLES I
This superb equestrian statue of Charles I was made by Hubert Le Sueur in 1633.
✚ G6 ✉ South side of Trafalgar Square 🚇 Charing Cross 🚇 Charing Cross

DUKE OF WELLINGTON
The only London hero to have three equestrian statues: the others are in St. Paul's Cathedral and outside the duke's home, Apsley House (➤ 52).
✚ J5 ✉ Opposite the Bank of England, EC2 🚇 Bank

EROS
Alfred Gilbert's memorial (1893) to the philanthropic 7th Earl of Shaftesbury (1801–85) actually portrays the Angel of Christian Charity, not Eros.
✚ F5 ✉ Piccadilly Circus, W1 🚇 Piccadilly Circus

MONUMENT
Wren's 202-foot Doric column commemorates the Great Fire (1666). Worth climbing the 311 steps for the view.
✚ K5 ✉ Monument Street, EC3 🚇 Monument

NELSON'S COLUMN
Horatio, Viscount Nelson (1758–1805) went up on to his 172-foot column in 1843; the hero died as he defeated the French and Spanish at Trafalgar.
✚ G6 ✉ Trafalgar Square 🚇 Charing Cross 🚇 Charing Cross

OLIVER CROMWELL
King-like Cromwell, Lord Protector of England from 1653 to 1658, looks across Parliament Square.
✚ G7 ✉ Houses of Parliament 🚇 Westminster

PETER PAN
George Frampton's statue (1912) of J. M. Barrie's creation, the boy who never grew up.
✚ C6 ✉ Long Water, Kensington Gardens 🚇 Lancaster Gate

QUEEN ALEXANDRA
This art nouveau bronze designed by Alfred Gilbert, a memorial to Edward VII's Danish-born wife, was commissioned by her daughter-in-law, Queen Mary.
✚ F6 ✉ Marlborough Road, SW1 🚇 Green Park

SIR ARTHUR SULLIVAN
William Goscombe John's bronze of the operetta composer Sir Arthur Sullivan (1842–1900).
✚ G5 ✉ Embankment Gardens 🚇 Embankment

The Broadgate Centre

Part of the rampant redevelopment of the City in the 1980s, Broadgate (➤ 54) was exceptional for its commissioning of public art. *Fulcrum*, by Richard Serra — vast steel sheets tentatively resting against each other, by Richard Serra, mark the Broadgate square entrance. Beyond are Barry Flanagan's *Leaping Hare on Crescent and Bell* and George Segal's *Rush Hour*. In the center of Broadgate is the circular Arena, which becomes an outdoor ice rink during the winter months. Encircling the Arena are chic restaurants, wine bars, and some shops.

Peter Pan, in Kensington Gardens

53

MODERN BUILDINGS

Designer store interiors

Sophisticated consumers have inspired retailers to create a stylish ambience in which to shop. Eva Jiricna has remodeled the Joseph shops (16 and 26 Sloane Street, SW1 and others) with her signature staircase, cable balustrades, and polished white plaster walls. Stanton Williams revamped Issey Miyake (270 Brompton Road, SW3), Branson Coates did Katharine Hamnett (20 Sloane Square, SW1) and Jigsaw (9 Argyll Street, W1 and others), and Wickham & Associates made Fifth Floor Harvey Nichols (➤ 71) a foodies' wonderland.

Broadgate

BROADGATE
This 29-acre mall and office development (1984–91) is distinguished by its impressive façades, large atria, open-air ice rink (winter), and lunchtime concerts in summer. The architects were Arup Associates, Skidmore, Owings & Merrill, Inc. See also panel page 53.
✚ K4 ✉ EC2 ☎ 0171-814 6638 🕒 24 hours 🍴 Many 🚇 Liverpool Street

CANARY WHARF TOWER
César Pelli's soaring, blue-topped tower, the first to be clad in stainless steel, dominates Canary Wharf; Pelli describes it as "a square prism with pyramidal top in the traditional form of the obelisk."
✉ 1, Canada Square, Canary Wharf, Isle of Dogs, E14 🕒 Public spaces are open, not buildings 🚇 Canary Wharf

EMBANKMENT PLACE: CHARING CROSS
Using the air rights above Charing Cross Station, Terry Farrell & Company created 355,000 square yards of office space between 1987 and 1990, suspended on bowstring arches.
✚ G6 ✉ Villiers Street, WC2 🕒 Public space 🍴 Many 🚇 Charing Cross

FINANCIAL TIMES PRINT WORKS
Built in a year in 1988, Nicholas Grimshaw and Partners' building is designed around two vast printing presses; printing can be watched through one huge window.
✉ 240 East India Dock Road, E14 🕒 No public access, but visit 9:30–2:30 and watch the presses running 🚇 All Saints

SACKLER GALLERIES
At Foster Associates' dazzling, airy rooftop galleries, light-sensitive louvers automatically control sunlight through fretted glass windows.
✚ F6 ✉ Royal Academy of Arts (➤ 51)

WATERLOO INTERNATIONAL STATION
Designed by Nicholas Grimshaw and Partners, this is one of the world's longest railroad stations, built to handle up to 15 million passengers a year; the viaduct structure for five new tracks is spanned by a dramatic, glazed bowstring arch.
✚ H6 ✉ SE1 🕒 Public space 🍴 Many 🚇 Waterloo

WEST ZENDERS
The latest glass curtain-wall technology made possible the building of Rick Mather's ultimate see-and-be-seen restaurant in 1991, where all three dining floors are visible from the street.
✚ G5 ✉ 4a Upper St. Martin's Lane, WC2 ☎ 0171-497 0376 🕒 Lunch, dinner 🍴 Bar, restaurant 🚇 Leicester Square

CHURCHES & CATHEDRALS

ALL-HALLOWS-BY-THE-TOWER
Begun about 1000, the church contains a Roman pavement and a carving by Grinling Gibbons.
➕ K5 ✉ Byward Street, EC3 ☎ 0171-481 2928 ⊕ Church Mon–Fri 9–6; Sat, Sun 10–5. Undercroft Museum: Mon–Sat 10–5, Sun 1–4:30 ⊜ Tower Hill ⊞ Museum donation requested

CHELSEA OLD CHURCH
Begun in 1157 but much rebuilt. One of the best series of monuments in a London parish church.
➕ D8 ✉ Old Church Street, SW3 ☎ 0171-352 7978 ⊕ Mon–Sat 10–1, 2–5; Sun 1:30–5 ⊜ Sloane Square ⊞ Free

ORATORY OF ST. PHILIP NERI
Also known as the Brompton or London Oratory; fine baroque inside.
➕ D7 ✉ Brompton Road, SW7 ☎ 0171-589 4811 ⊕ Daily 6:30–8 ⊜ South Kensington ⊞ Free

ST. ETHELDREDA'S CHAPEL
This Gothic chapel survives from the Bishops of Ely's medieval townhouse.
➕ H4 ✉ Ely Place, EC1 ☎ 0171-405 1061 ⊕ Daily 7:30–7 ⊜ Chancery Lane, Farringdon 🚇 Farringdon ⊞ Free

ST JAMES'S, PICCADILLY
Wren's chic church (1682–84) for local aristocracy has a sumptuous interior.
➕ F6 ✉ Piccadilly, SW1 ☎ 0171-734 4511 ⊕ Daily 8:30–7 🍴 Café ⊜ Piccadilly Circus ⊞ Free

ST. MARGARET, LOTHBURY
Wren's church (1686–90) retains its huge carved screen with soaring eagle and carved pulpit tester.
➕ J5 ✉ Lothbury, EC2 ☎ 0171-606 8330 ⊕ Mon–Fri 8–5 ⊜ Bank ⊞ Free

TEMPLE CHURCH
Begun about 1160, the circular plan was inspired by Jerusalem's Dome of the Rock. Effigies in the nave honor the Knights Templar, protectors of pilgrims to the Holy Land.
➕ H5 ✉ Inner Temple, EC4 ☎ 0171-353 1736 ⊕ Wed–Sun 10–4 ⊜ Temple ⊞ Free

Chapels Royal
London's five Chapels Royal are at St. James's Palace, Queen's Chapel, the Tower (St. Peter ad Vincula and St. John's) and Hampton Court Palace. The best services to attend are at St. Peter ad Vincula, St. James's Palace and Hampton Court, as each retains a lavish, courtly atmosphere and has a superb choir.

The Oratory of St. Philip Neri (Brompton Oratory), by Herbert Gribble (1876)

GREEN SPACES

London is almost 11 percent parkland and has 67 square miles of green space, including the nine royal parks, former royal hunting grounds.

See Top 25 Sights for
HAMPSTEAD HEATH(➤29)
KENSINGTON GARDENS (➤25)
REGENT'S PARK (➤30)
ROYAL BOTANICAL GARDENS, KEW (➤24)
ST. JAMES'S PARK (➤33)

BUNHILL FIELDS
Leafy City oasis, where trees shade the tombs of Blake and Defoe.
✚ J4 ✉ City Road, EC1 ☎ 0171-332 1456 ⏰ Mon–Fri 7:30–7:30; Sat, Sun 9:30–4 🚇 Old Street 💷 Free

Riders in Rotten Row, Hyde Park

GREEN PARK
Peaceful royal park.
✚ F6 ✉ SW1 ☎ 0171-930 1793 ⏰ Daily dawn–dusk 🚇 Green Park, Hyde Park Corner 💷 Free

GREENWICH ➤20

HOLLAND PARK
Woodland and open lawns fill 54 acres around Holland House.
✚ A6 ✉ W11 ☎ 0171-602 2226 ⏰ Daily 8–dusk 🍴 Restaurant, café 🚇 Holland Park 💷 Free

HOLY TRINITY, BROMPTON
A large, tree-shaded, airy churchyard, useful between South Kensington Museum visits.
✚ D7 ✉ Brompton Road, SW7 ⏰ 24 hours 🚇 South Kensington 💷 Free

HYDE PARK
One of London's largest open spaces, tamed by Queen Caroline's gardener.
✚ D6 ✉ W2 ☎ 0171-298 2100 ⏰ Daily 5–midnight 🍴 Restaurant, café 🚇 Marble Arch, Lancaster Gate, Knightsbridge, Hyde Park Corner 💷 Free

PRIMROSE HILL
One of London's best panoramas.
✚ D2 ✉ NW3 ☎ 0171-486 7905 ⏰ 24 hours 🚇 St. John's Wood, Camden Town 💷 Free

RUSSELL SQUARE
Lawns, trees and café near the British Museum.
✚ G4 ✉ WC1 ⏰ Daily 7–dusk 🍴 Café 🚇 Russell Square 💷 Free

Royal parks

The nine royal parks, mostly former hunting grounds, are Londoners' substitute backyards. They also act as the city's green lungs. Many are also important bird sanctuaries. Their open spaces, woods, meadows, ponds, and wide variety of mature trees have been the setting for events ranging from the Great Exhibition of 1851 to riotous demonstrations. Today, they are places to meet, picnic, play games and, in summer, enjoy a concert or a play.

THAMES SIGHTS

London grew up around the Thames. As the port expanded, so did London's wealth and power. The Thames was its main thoroughfare, used by all.

BAZALGETTE'S EMBANKMENT ➤12

CLEOPATRA'S NEEDLE
The 86-foot-tall pink granite obelisk made in 1450 BC records the triumphs of Rameses the Great.
➕ G6 ✉ Victoria Embankment, WC2 🚇 Embankment, Charing Cross Pier 🎫 Free

DOCKLANDS
Waterparks, the high level Docklands Light Railway, Island Gardens and ambitious buildings.
✉ LDDC Visitors Centre, 3 Limeharbour, E14 ☎ 0171-512 111
🕐 Mon–Fri 8:30–6; Sat, Sun 9:30–5. Closed Dec 25–26
🚉 Crossharbour DLR 🎫 Free

DRAGONS ON EMBANKMENT
The silver cast-iron dragons (1849) mark the border between the cities of London and Westminster.
➕ H5 ✉ Victoria Embankment, WC2 🚇 Temple
🎫 Free

SMUGGLERS' PUBS, WAPPING
The Town of Ramsgate and Prospect of Whitby are atmospheric smugglers' pubs.
➕ L6 ✉ Wapping, E1 ☎ Town of Ramsgate 0171-488 2685; Prospect of Whitby 0171-481 1095
🕐 Mon–Sat 11:30AM–11PM; Sun 12–3, 7–10:30
🍴 Bar food 🚇 Wapping 🚉 Limehouse DLR

TOWER BRIDGE MUSEUM
Opened in 1894; fine views from the museum and catwalk between the towers; engine rooms at the south bank end.
➕ K6 ✉ SE1 ☎ 0171-407 0922 🕐 Apr–Oct, daily 10:30–6:30; Nov–Mar, daily 10–5:15 (last admission 75 mins before closing). Closed Dec 25–26, Jan 1, Good Fri
🚶 Tower Hill to Tower Pier 🎫 Expensive

WATERLOO BRIDGE
Gilbert Scott's cantilevered concrete; superb views.
➕ H6 ✉ WC2 🚇 Waterloo 🚶 Waterloo to Charing Cross Pier

Riverboats
On a sunny day take the Underground to Westminster and catch a riverboat up or down the Thames for the morning. Trips downstream pass Westminster, the City, and Docklands, stopping at Charing Cross, Tower, and Greenwich piers. A longer trip upstream meanders past London's villages, stopping at Putney Bridge, Kew, Richmond, and Hampton Court piers.

The Prospect of Whitby, an old riverside smugglers' pub in Wapping

CHILDREN'S FAVORITES

Backstage tours

Going behind the scenes is great fun. In London, there are some fun backstage tours. See how the scenery, props, and costumes are made at the National Theatre (➤ 79), or explore backstage at the Royal Shakespeare Company's Barbican and Pit theaters (➤ 79). Or you can have the crowds cheer for you when you visit Wembley Stadium (➤ 83).

Children are likely to enjoy almost everything in London, provided it is made to be fun and does not last too long. See London's Top 25 sights (➤ 24–28) for other ideas. Here are some special outings that should appeal particularly to younger visitors.

BETHNAL GREEN MUSEUM OF CHILDHOOD

This outpost of the Victoria & Albert Museum (➤ 28) is an enormous train shed packed with Noah's arks, dolls, toy soldiers, puppets, and even a model circus.

✚ M3 ✉ Cambridge Heath Road, E2 ☎ 0181-980 3204 Mon–Thu, Sat 10–5:50; Sun 2:30–5:50. Closed Dec 25 🍴 Café 🚇 Bethnal Green 🚉 Bethnal Green 💷 Free

GUINNESS WORLD OF RECORDS

It's great fun to listen to the man who hiccuped longest, to meet current world achievers, to compare your own shoe size with the tallest man's footprint, and much more.

✚ F5 ✉ The Trocadero, Piccadilly Circus, W1 ☎ 0171-439 7331 🕐 Daily 10–10. Closed Dec 25 🚇 Piccadilly Circus 💷 Expensive; family ticket

HAMLEYS

Central London's biggest toy shop, a seven-floor wonderland where if you do not manage to find what you want you will just have to go home and make it.

✚ F5 ✉ 188 Regent Street, W1 ☎ 0171-734 3161 🕐 Mon–Fri 10–7, Thu 10–8, Sat 9:30–7, Sun 12–6. Closed Dec 25 and occasional Suns 🍴 Café 🚇 Oxford Circus 💷 Free

H.M.S. *BELFAST*

You will need to put aside two hours to clamber up, down, and around this 1938 war cruiser, visiting the cabins, gun turrets, bridge, and boiler-room.

✚ K6 ✉ Morgan's Lane, Tooley Street, SE1 ☎ 0171-407 6434 🕐 Mar–Oct, daily 10–6; Nov–Feb, daily 10–5. Closed Dec 24–26 🍴 Café 🚇 London Bridge 🚉 London Bridge 💷 Moderate; family tickets

Model theaters in Pollock Toy Musuem

LONDON DUNGEON

Among the musty smells and eerie screams lurk torture chambers, Jack the Ripper, and London's grizzliest moments relived, some using rather disturbing sound effects.

✚ K6 ✉ 28–34 Tooley Street, SE1 ☎ 0171-403 0606 🕐 Daily 10–5:30 (last admission 4:30). Closed Dec 25 🍴 Restaurant, café 🚇 London Bridge 🚉 London Bridge 💷 Very expensive

MADAME TUSSAUD'S AND THE LONDON PLANETARIUM

Madame Tussaud learned the art of waxworks from her uncle; see how many people you can identify, from Shakespeare to Madonna, and do not miss the Spirit of London ride. The revamped Planetarium has a new star show and interactive exhibition area.

E4 ⊠ Marylebone Road, W1 ☎ 0171-935 6861 ⏰ May–Sep, daily 9–5:30; Oct–Jun, Mon–Fri 10–5:30, Sat, Sun 9:30–5:30. Planetarium closed schoolday mornings. Closed Dec 25 🍴 Restaurant, café 🚇 Baker Street ⚡ Very expensive; family ticket; combined ticket with Planetarium. Discount tickets for Rock Circus (see below) available here

OPEN TOP BUS: LONDON PLUS

Cruise about town on an open-topped double decker bus marked "Hop-on hop-off"; tickets and route maps available on board.

Moves around Central London ⊠ Pick-up points include Victoria Street, Haymarket, Marble Arch, with stops in between ☎ 0181-877 1722 ⏰ 10–4 🚇 See above ⚡ Very expensive, valid all day (or a day and a half if bought after lunch); family tickets

POLLOCK TOY MUSEUM

Two houses full of dolls, teddy bears, puppets, and Mr. Pollock's workshop where he made his toy theaters—still sold at the shop.

F4 ⊠ 1 Scala Street, W1 ☎ 0171-636 3452 ⏰ Mon–Sat 10–5. Closed Dec 24–26, Jan 1, Bank holidays 🚇 Goodge Street ⚡ Cheap

ROCK CIRCUS

Rock legends past and present seem to come alive when visitors' headphones pick up infra-red signals and play their songs.

F5 ⊠ London Pavilion, Piccadilly Circus, W1 ☎ 0171-734 7203 ⏰ Sun–Thu 11–9; Fri, Sat 11–10; 10–10 during school vacation. Closed Dec 25 🚇 Piccadilly Circus ⚡ Very expensive; family ticket. Discount tickets for Madame Tussaud's (see above) available here

TOWER HILL PAGEANT

A time car glides slowly past 26 tableaux of London, giving its sounds, smells and history, and providing an excellent introduction to the City.

K5 ⊠ 1 Tower Hill, Terrace, EC3 ☎ 0171-709 0081 ⏰ Apr–Oct, daily 9:30–5:50, (until 6 in Aug); Nov–Mar, daily 9:30–4:30. Closed Dec 25 🚇 Tower Hill Riverboat to Tower Pier ⚡ Expensive; family ticket

TOY WORLD, HARRODS

Up on the fourth floor, every child's dream outing to paradise; plenty of toys to play with – and perhaps one to buy.

D7 ⊠ Brompton Road, SW1 ☎ 0171-730 1234 ⏰ Mon–Fri 10–6, Wed–Fri until 7. Closed Sun 🍴 Restaurants, cafés 🚇 Knightsbridge ⚡ Free

Harrods—an outing in itself

London for free

London has plenty of free activities for all ages. Several public galleries are free (National Gallery ➤ 39, National Portrait Gallery ➤ 38, Tate Gallery, free except for special exhibitions, ➤ 34) plus the commercial ones (➤ 72). Many museums are free (British Museum ➤ 43, Wallace Collection, Bank of England ➤ 50–51) and music can be enjoyed in church concerts, pubs, and arts complexes. For free theater, try an art auction (➤ 72), a debate in Parliament (➤ 36) or a B.B.C. recording session (☎ 0181-743 8000 and ask for ticket enquiries, specifying radio or TV).

HIDDEN LONDON

Cricket

Anyone who watches or plays cricket should visit the M.C.C. Museum hidden away at Lord's. The story of the game is told in pictures, cartoons, and old battered bats; the Ashes are kept here, too. It is open to ticket-holders on match days, while at other times the guided tour includes the Long Room and the beautiful new stand designed by Michael Hopkins in 1985–87.

➕ D3

✉ Marylebone Cricket Club, Lord's Ground, NW8

☎ 0171-289 1611; tour bookings 0171-266 3825

⏰ Guided tours noon and 2, daily; 10AM, noon and 2 on match days

🚇 St. John's Wood

💷 Expensive

Chelsea Pensioners, residents of the Royal Hospital, Chelsea

See Top 25 Sights for
BANQUETING HOUSE (▶37)

CHELSEA PHYSIC GARDEN
Sir Hans Sloane laid out this walled garden for the Society of Apothecaries in 1673.
➕ D8 ✉ Swan Walk, SW3 ☎ 0171-352 5646 ⏰ April–Oct, Wed 2–5, Sun 2–6. 🍴 Tea available 🚇 Sloane Square 💷 Moderate

DULWICH PICTURE GALLERY ▶50

INNER AND MIDDLE TEMPLE
These two Inns of Court are named after the Knights Templar, whose church (▶55) is here, too.
➕ H5 ✉ Middle Temple, Middle Temple Lane, EC4 ☎ 0171-353 4355 ⏰ Middle Temple Hall: Mon–Fri 10–noon, 3–4 (phone first). Closed Easter, Whitsun, Aug and Christmas 🚇 Temple 💷 Free

ROYAL HOSPITAL, CHELSEA
Wren's 1682 building, inspired by the Hôtel des Invalides in Paris, is still a home for veteran soldiers.
➕ E8 ✉ Royal Hospital Road, SW3 ☎ 0171-730 0161 ⏰ Museum, Great Hall and Chapel: Mon–Fri 10–noon, 2–4; Sat 2–4. Closed Bank holidays and May 15–end Jun 🚇 Sloane Square 💷 Free

ST. DUNSTAN IN THE EAST
Wren's 1698 tower soars above a secret garden.
➕ K5 ✉ St. Dunstan's Hill, EC3 ⏰ Mon–Fri dawn–dusk 🚇 Monument, Tower Hill 💷 Free

ST. ETHELDREDA'S ▶55

ST. GEORGE, HANOVER SQUARE GARDENS
Tree-shaded oasis in Mayfair.
➕ E5 ✉ Enter from South Audley Street and Mount Street, W1 🚇 Bond Street, Green Park 💷 Free

SUTTON HOUSE
Tudor house (1535) with linen-fold paneling and wall-paintings.
➕ M1 ✉ 2 & 4 Homerton Street, E9 ☎ 0181-986 2264 ⏰ Feb–Nov, Wed, Sun; Bank holiday Mon 11:30–5; mid-Apr–Oct, 2–5. Late opening July, Wed, Fri 7– 9:30. Closed Sat Oct 14–Nov 🍴 Café 🚇 Homerton 💷 Cheap

TEMPLE OF MITHRAS
The ground floor of this Roman temple survives.
➕ J5 ✉ Bucklersbury, EC4 ⏰ 24 hours 🚇 Bank 💷 Free

LONDON
where to...

BRASSERIES & BRUNCH

The cost of a meal

Eating out in London is generally expensive and prices vary widely. The restaurants on the following pages are in three categories:

£££ from £30 per person, without drinks

££ from £20 per person, without drinks

£ from £10 per person, without drinks

In addition, expect to pay service charges (usually 12.5 per cent) and sometimes cover charges (£1.50 per person) as well.

Museum restaurants

Museum restaurants have improved hugely over recent years. The best are the Tate Restaurant (➤ 34), the Blue Print above the Design Museum (➤ 50) or, simpler, the National Gallery's Brasserie (➤ 39) overlooking Trafalgar Square. The Museum of Mankind has Café de Colombia (➤ 51), the Royal Academy has its restaurant decorated by Academicians (➤ 51); Chiswick House has Burlington Café (➤ 52) and Kensington Palace offers the ultimate tea in its magnificent Orangery (➤ 25).

THE BOX (£)
Popular café whose food ranges from bruschetta pissaladière to smoked chicken and a good tarte au citron; jazz for Sun brunch.
➕ G5 ✉ 32–34 Monmouth Street, WC2 ☎ 0171-240 5828 ⏰ Lunch, tea, dinner, Sun brunch

LA BRASSERIE (££)
Very French and usually very full of Chelsea and Fulham locals on shopping trips; Sunday brunch is an institution.
➕ D7 ✉ 272 Brompton Road, SW3 ☎ 0171-584 1668 ⏰ Breakfast, lunch, tea, dinner

BRASSERIE DU MARCHÉ AUX PUCES (££)
At the north end of Portobello Road, ideal after Portobello Market's excitements.
➕ B5 ✉ 349 Portobello Road, W10 ☎ 0181-968 5828 ⏰ Lunch, dinner. Closed Sun, Mon

LA BRASSERIE ST. QUENTIN (££)
Uncompromisingly French with a Parisian interior, ideal for an indulgent break from a South Kensington museums day.
➕ D7 ✉ 243 Brompton Road, SW3 ☎ 0171-581 5131 ⏰ Lunch, dinner

CAMDEN BRASSERIE (££)
Good for grilled steak, *frites* and a bottle of wine after Camden Lock markets; Underground Café is downstairs.
➕ F2 ✉ 214–216 Camden High Street, NW1 ☎ 0171-482 2114 ⏰ Lunch, dinner, Sun brunch

CHRISTOPHER'S (££)
One of the best London haunts for a genuine American brunch, and in one of London's most beautiful dining-rooms.
➕ G5 ✉ 18 Wellington Street, WC2 ☎ 0171-240 4222 ⏰ Lunch, dinner, Sun brunch

GRILL ST QUENTIN (££)
Good atmosphere in this huge basement where a bowl of *frites* is essential; cheap pre-8PM menu.
➕ D7 ✉ 2 Yeoman's Row, SW3 ☎ 0171-581 8377 ⏰ Lunch, dinner

JOE ALLEN (££)
A dependably convivial, club-like atmosphere, with healthy American Cal-Ital food served by smiling waiters; reservations essential.
➕ G5 ✉ 13 Exeter Street, WC2 ☎ 0171-836 0651/497 2148 ⏰ Lunch, dinner

SMOLLENSKY'S ON THE STRAND (££)
The large bar is one of London's best; steaks are the thing to eat; cheap pre-6PM menu.
➕ G5 ✉ 105 The Strand, WC2 ☎ 0171-497 2101/836 3270 ⏰ Lunch, tea, dinner, Sun brunch

WINDOWS ON THE WORLD (£££)
The view is included in the price, as is the skill of chef David Chambers. On a clear day brunch here is memorable.
➕ E6 ✉ The Hilton Hotel, 22 Park Lane, W1 ☎ 0171-493 8000 ⏰ Lunch, dinner, Sun brunch

SHOPS & PUBS

CAFÉ AT HEAL'S (££)

Ambrose Heal's store, which promotes vernacular furniture, keeps design as high priority in the café, too; book for lunch.

✚ F4 ✉ 196 Tottenham Court Road, W1 ☎ 0171-636 1666
🕔 Lunch, tea

THE EAGLE (£)

This, the first of London's new-wave pubs, serves robust, Mediterranean food to a noisy full house.

✚ H4 ✉ 159 Farringdon Road, EC1 ☎ 0171-837 1353
🕔 Lunch, dinner. Closed Sat, Sun

FIFTH FLOOR AT HARVEY NICHOLS (££)

Henry Harris cooks modern British cuisine for a chic clientele in Julian Wickham's designer room. For the less well-heeled, there are cafés outside the restaurant and down in the basement.

✚ E6 ✉ Knightsbridge, SW1 ☎ 0171-235 5250 🕔 Lunch, dinner

HARRODS (£–££)

Each day, 12 eateries swing into action. The best are the Health Juice Bar (basement); the Salt Beef Bar, Champagne and Oyster Bar, Café Espresso, and Bar à Fromage (first floor), the Georgian Restaurant and Terrace Bar (good for traditional tea) and the Ice-cream Parlour and Upper Circle Self-Service.

✚ D7 ✉ Knightsbridge, SW1 ☎ 0171-730 1234
🕔 Breakfast, lunch, tea

LAMB TAVERN (£)

Regulars claim this restored Victorian pub in the Leadenhall Market serves the best hot roast beef sandwiches in the City.

✚ K5 ✉ 10–12 Leadenhall Market, EC3 ☎ 0171-626 2454
🕔 Lunch. Closed Sat, Sun

LIBERTY'S (£–££)

It is almost a meal just feasting on the goods in this exotic store; in case not, the stylish ABC Café is the best of three options.

✚ F5 ✉ 214–22 Regent Street, W1 ☎ 0171-734 1234
🕔 Breakfast, lunch, tea

NEWMAN ARMS (£)

The pie room upstairs is what this pub is all about, with fillings ranging from steak and kidney and fish to lamb and rosemary; the salads are equally delicious.

✚ F4 ✉ 23 Rathbone Street, W1 ☎ 0171-636 1127
🕔 Mon–Fri lunch

PEASANT (£)

Still feels like a pub, but touched with the wand of a design-conscious foodie. Carla Tomasi's modern Italian food is excellent.

✚ H4 ✉ 240 St. John Street, EC1 ☎ 0171-336 7726
🕔 Lunch, dinner. Closed Sat lunch, Sun

SCARSDALE (£)

Pretty Kensington pub with a garden overlooking the Square, serving traditional pub food to all who can find a seat inside or out.

✚ B7 ✉ 23a Edwardes Square, W8 ☎ 0171-937 1811
🕔 Lunch, dinner

Fish restaurants

London does not abound in good fish restaurants. For traditional fish try Sweetings in the City (39 Queen Victoria Street) or Bill Bentley's (31 Beauchamp Place, SW3 and others). (The English oyster season covers all the months with 'r' in them.) Green's Restaurant and Oyster Bar (36 Duke Street, St. James's) and the very jolly Manzi's (➤ 86) are less formal. L'Altro (➤ 68) and Sheekey's Brasserie annex, Josef (28 St. Martin's Court), have lighter cooking. For good fish and chips, try Wilton Road, behind Victoria Station.

BREAKFAST & TEA

Set-price menus

Most of London's pricier restaurants offer two set-price menus, the cheaper at lunchtime. Stick to them and you can savor sublime dishes. Consider dressing up to try classic Anglo-French cuisine at the exquisite Connaught Grill (➤ 69), or spend an afternoon lunching at Pierre Koffman's La Tante Claire (68 Royal Hospital Road, SW3). All the star chefs do it, from Nico (Nico at Ninety, 90 Park Lane, W1) and Alastair Little (➤ 69) to Gordon Ramsay (➤ 65).

The check

A good-value menu can be transformed into an outrageous check if you do not look sharp. Check beforehand whether or not service, VAT and coffee are included, and order tap water if you do not want to pay for bottled. When the check arrives, check it carefully. If service is already added, you are not obliged to leave a tip, even if the waiter looks hopeful.

BLAKES HOTEL (££)
Anouska Hempel's seductively romantic décor and ambience makes this the perfect place for superb breakfast or tea à deux.
➕ C8 ✉ 33 Roland Gardens, SW7 ☎ 0171-370 6701
⊕ Breakfast, tea

CLARIDGES (££)
Breakfast is in the immaculate art deco restaurant; tea, the best in London, is taken on sofas in the foyer alcove—reservations essential.
➕ E5 ✉ Brook Street, W1 ☎ 0171-629 8860
⊕ Breakfast, tea. Dress code: jacket and tie

COFFEE GALLERY (£)
Italian-run café, ideal for pre-British Museum coffee and croissants, and post-museum pasta and wicked cakes.
➕ G5 ✉ 23 Museum Street, WC1 ☎ 0171-436 0455
⊕ Breakfast, tea. Closed Sun

FOX AND ANCHOR (£)
Join Smithfield meat market workers for a full English breakfast washed down with coffee (or a pint). Best value in town.
➕ J4 ✉ 115 Charterhouse Street, EC1 ☎ 0171-253 4838
⊕ Breakfast. Closed Sun

HYDE PARK HOTEL (££)
Reserve a window table in the Park Room for a calm, stylish breakfast or tea overlooking Hyde Park.
➕ E6 ✉ Knightsbridge, SW1 ☎ 0171-235 2000
⊕ Breakfast, tea

MAISON MALINOWSKI (£)
The ultimate designer café: distressed walls, minimalist tables and superb croissants, cakes and quiches.
➕ G5 ✉ 63 Neal Street, WC2 ☎ 0171-836 9779

PÂTISSERIE VALERIE (£)
Coffee, croissants, cakes at tiny tables; compete with regulars for a seat. Branches at Covent Garden, Russell Street, Brompton Roads and Marylebone High Street.
➕ F5 ✉ 44 Old Compton Street, W1 ☎ 0171-437 3466
⊕ Breakfast, tea

SAVOY HOTEL (££)
Book a window table for breakfast in the River Room; tea is on sofas in the pretty Thames Foyer.
➕ G5 ✉ Strand, WC2 ☎ 0171-836 4343
⊕ Breakfast, tea. Dress code: jacket and tie

SIMPSON'S-IN-THE-STRAND (££)
Glorious setting for a traditional breakfast—such as porridge followed by kippers or kidneys.
➕ G5 ✉ 100 Strand, WC2 ☎ 0171-836 9112
⊕ Breakfast, tea. Dress code: jacket and tie

WALDORF (££)
Breakfast in the lofty Palm Court is buffet style, with a flagon of fresh juice at the table; tea is traditional, with weekend tea-dances.
➕ G5 ✉ Aldwych, WC2 ☎ 0171-836 2400
⊕ Breakfast, tea. Dress code: jacket and tie for tea-dance

FAMOUS CHEFS

JOËL ANTUNÈS, LES SAVEURS (£££)
Superlative French food served in a room totally devoid of atmosphere.
➕ E6 ✉ 37a Curzon Street, W1 ☎ 0171-491 8919 🕐 Lunch, dinner. Closed Sat, Sun. Dress code: jacket & tie

BRUNO LOUBET, BISTROT BRUNO (££)
Bruno Loubet and Pierre Condou's inventive dishes served in chic, cramped surroundings.
➕ F5 ✉ 63 Frith Street, W1 ☎ 0171-734 4545 🕐 Lunch, dinner. Closed Sat lunch, Sun lunch, dinner

JEAN-CHRISTOPHE NOVELLI, FOUR SEASONS (£££)
A rather stiff atmosphere; currently considered the best French food in town.
➕ E6 ✉ Four Seasons Hotel, W1 ☎ 0171-499 0888 🕐 Lunch, dinner. Dress code: jacket

GORDON RAMSAY, AUBERGINE (£££)
French food that uses ingredients like truffle oil over the haricots blancs; restful, book in advance.
➕ C8 ✉ 11 Park Walk, SW10 ☎ 0171-352 3449 🕐 Lunch, dinner. Closed Sat lunch, Sun lunch, dinner

MARCO PIERRE WHITE, HYDE PARK HOTEL (£££)
Now ensconced in posh Knightsbridge, the *enfant terrible* harasses his clients less—but still cooks wonderfully.
➕ E6 ✉ 66 Knightsbridge, SW1Y E6 ☎ 0171-235 2000/259 5380 🕐 Lunch, dinner

RICHARD CORRIGAN, FULHAM ROAD (£££)
Corrigan, a Stephen Bull protégé, creates masterly modern British dishes—many of them using his favorite ingredient, offal.
➕ C8 ✉ 257–9 Fulham Road, SW3 ☎ 0171-351 7823 🕐 Lunch, dinner

ROBERT GUTTERIDGE, ALFRED (££)
Dramatic contemporary interior, the best selection of bottled British beers and rehabilitated English dishes, such as rabbit and toad-in-the-hole.
➕ G5 ✉ 245 Shaftesbury Avenue, W1 ☎ 0171-240 2566 🕐 Lunch, dinner. Closed Sun

ROWLEY LEIGH, KENSINGTON PLACE (££)
Top-notch food at reasonable prices in west London's noisiest, jolliest and fullest upmarket social restaurant.
➕ B6 ✉ 201–5 Kensington Church Street, W8 ☎ 0171-727 3184 🕐 Lunch, dinner

RUTH ROGERS AND ROSE GRAY, RIVER CAFÉ (£££)
Outstanding modern Italian food in Richard Rogers's refurbished room with a 50-foot-long stainless steel bar.
✉ Thames Wharf, Rainville Road, W6 ☎ 0171-381 8824 🕐 Lunch, dinner. Closed Sun dinner

Riverside eating
London has only recently cottoned on to the potential of its riverside views. Until recently, the only places where you could eat with a view were the grand Savoy River Room (➤ 64) and the East End smugglers' pubs (➤ 57). Today there is a choice. The top river view is from the first-floor designer restaurant, Blue Print Café, in the Design Museum, Butler's Wharf, overlooking Tower Bridge and the City. Near by, Cantina de Ponte's views are second best on the south bank (Shad Thames, SE1). For more modest river-view eating, try Embankment Tea House, on a mound in Victoria Embankment Gardens, and Barley Mow pub, 44 Narrow Street, E14, whose outdoor tables overlook the wider, curving Thames of the East End.

65

CHINESE & FAR EASTERN RESTAURANTS

Best settings

If part of the pleasure of dining out is the setting, London has much to offer. For grandeur, there's the Ritz (➤ 84) at lunchtime; for sparkle, the mosaic-clad Criterion (Piccadilly); for art deco, Claridge's (➤ 84); for *fin de siècle*, the Café Royal (Regent Street, W1 ✚ F5). There are whacky settings, such as Balti's (➤ 67), the Dorchester's pricey Oriental and the Star of India (Park Lane, W1 ✚ 6E). And there are atmospheric pubs such as the George Inn (77 Borough High Street, SE1 ✚ J6), architects' dreams such as the River Café (Thames Wharf Studios, Rainville Road, W6) and the most beautiful walls at Christopher's (➤ 62).

ABENO (££)

A ten-minute walk from Colindale Underground station, this *okonomi-yaki* (mini-pizzas cooked on a griddle) restaurant is in Europe's only Japanese shopping plaza.
✉ Yaohan Plaza, 339 Edgware Road, NW9 ☎ 0181-205 1131
◉ Lunch, dinner

BAHN THAI (££)

The finest Thai cooking in London, for authenticity and price; reserve a table on the first floor.
✚ F5 ✉ 21a Frith Street, W1
☎ 0171-437 8504 ◉ Lunch, dinner

CHURCHILL ARMS (£)

London's first pub to serve good, inexpensive Thai food. Best to book.
✚ B6 ✉ 119 Kensington Church Street, W8
☎ 0171-792 1246 ◉ Lunch, dinner. Closed Sun dinner

HARBOUR CITY (£)

Great dim sum in a highly reputed Soho Chinese restaurant.
✚ G5 ✉ 46 Gerrard Street, W1 ☎ 0171-439 7859
◉ Lunch, dinner

IMPERIAL CITY (££)

Good Chinese food in the Royal Exchange vaults.
✚ K5 ✉ Royal Exchange, Cornhill, EC3 ☎ 0171-626 3437
◉ Lunch, dinner. Closed Sat, Sun

MANOROM (£)

Unusually for Covent Garden, this small, efficient restaurant serves good food at low prices; keep off the set-price menu.
✚ G5 ✉ 16 Maiden Lane, WC2 ☎ 0171-240 4139
◉ Lunch, dinner. Closed Sat lunch, Sun

NOTO RAMEN HOUSE (££)

Authentic Japanese ramen bar in the City with plastic models of the dishes outside. Conveniently located for the Barbican.
✚ J5 ✉ Bow Bells House, 7 Bread Street, EC4 ☎ 0171-329 8056 ◉ Lunch, dinner. Closed Sat dinner, Sun

ROYAL CHINA (££)

Book a table or join the justifiably long lines for the best dim sum in town.
✚ C5 ✉ 13 Queensway, W2
☎ 0171-221 2535 ◉ Lunch, dinner. No booking Sat, Sun

SINGAPORE GARDEN (££)

A favorite with north Londoners, and always packed, for its Malaysian and Indonesian seasonal specialties. Branch in Gloucester Place.
✚ C2 ✉ 83–83a Fairfax Road, NW6 ☎ 0171-328 5314
◉ Lunch, dinner

SRI SIAM (££)

A popular good-value, Thai restaurant in Soho. Their City branch, Sri Siam City, on London Wall, is in a stylish basement.
✚ F5 ✉ 14 Old Compton Street, W1 ☎ 0171-434 3544
◉ Lunch, dinner. Closed Sun lunch

WAGAMAMA (£)

London's trendiest Japanese ramen bar, convenient for the British Museum.
✚ G5 ✉ 4 Streatham Street, WC1 ☎ 0171-323 9223
◉ Lunch, dinner. No booking

INDIAN & VEGETARIAN RESTAURANTS

BALTI'S (£)

Bring your own alcohol to this luxurious building/health spa, and eat trendy Indian food cooked in *karahis* (iron dishes).

➕ C7 ✉ The London Esthetique, 41 Queen's Gate Terrace, SW7 ☎ 0171-581 3019 🕐 Dinner only. Closed Sun; bring your own alcohol

CARNEVALE (£)

Modern café near the Barbican, serving high quality vegetables, delicious breads, home-made lemonade—and wine, too.

➕ J4 ✉ 135 Whitecross Street, EC1 ☎ 0171-250 3452 🕐 Lunch, dinner (closes 9PM). Closed Sat, Sun

CHUTNEY MARY (££)

Try unusual Indian recipes that Indian chefs used to cook for the British on the sub-continent.

➕ C9 ✉ 535 King's Road, SW10 ☎ 0171-351 3113 🕐 Lunch, dinner. Sun buffet lunch

COUNTRY LIFE (£)

The Seventh Day Adventists run this plain basement restaurant, serving good, cheap food.

➕ F5 ✉ 1 Heddon Street, W1 ☎ 0171-434 2922 🕐 Lunch Sun–Fri; dinner Tue–Thu, Sun

CRANKS (£)

The mother of London veggie restaurants and one of a chain serving good value, good quality food.

➕ F5 ✉ 8 Marshall Street, W1 ☎ 0171-437 9431 🕐 Breakfast, lunch, dinner (closes 8–9PM). Closed Sun

DIWANA BHEL POORI HOUSE (£)

Bhel poori are fried snacks sold on the Bombay streets and beaches; in this vegetarian restaurant, they are served as first courses.

➕ F4 ✉ 121 Drummond Street, NW1 ☎ 0171-387 5556 🕐 Lunch, dinner. Lunch buffet; no booking; for dinner bring your own alcohol

NAMASTE (£)

A reward for hours spent in the food-free Tower of London, Cyrus Todiwala's food is unusually good.

➕ L5 ✉ 30 Alie Street, E1 ☎ 0171-488 9242/9339 🕐 Lunch, dinner. Closed Sat lunch, Sun lunch, dinner

NEAL'S YARD DINING ROOM (£)

A fresh, modern approach to vegetarian food with Indian, Mexican, Greek, and Turkish influences.

➕ G5 ✉ First floor, 14 Neal's Yard, WC2 ☎ 0171-379 0298 🕐 Mon–Sat lunch; Wed–Fri dinner until 8PM (except Thu in winter); no booking; bring your own alcohol

SALLOOS (££)

Upmarket, good North-West Frontier food for meat-eaters, cooked under the auspices of Mr. Salahuddin of Lahore.

➕ E6 ✉ 62–64 Kinnerton Street, SW1 ☎ 0171-235 4444/6845 🕐 Lunch, dinner. Closed Sun dinner

SWEET AND SPICY (£)

Basic cafeteria-style eatery serving Pakistani food, mostly to local Bangladeshis.

➕ L4 ✉ 42 Brick Lane, E1 ☎ 0171-247 1081 🕐 Breakfast, lunch, tea, dinner

Indian food

An Indian meal should have many dishes, so if there is a group of you it is best to make a collective order and share. Tandoori dishes (cooked in a clay oven) make a good start. The main course dishes should arrive together: one or two meat, two or three vegetable, a lentil or pulse dish (such as chickpea), rice and a variety of breads such as chapati or nan—which are eaten hot, so order more as you go along. Remember the yogurt and pickles, and drink lassi (a buttermilk or yogurt drink that comes in sweet or salty versions) or beer.

ITALIAN & FRENCH RESTAURANTS

American food

America's fast-food arrived long before its quality cuisine and restaurant style. The newer arrivals have made up for lost time and there are now plenty of places to hang out: The Hard Rock Café (150 Old Park Lane, W1), Kenny's (2a Pond Place, SW3), Rock Island Diner (Plaza Centre, London Pavilion, Piccadilly), Planet Hollywood (Trocadero Centre, Coventry Street, W1), Fatboy's Diner (21 Maiden Lane, WC2), Chicago Pizza Pie Factory (17 Hanover Square, W1), TGIF (6 Bedford Street and branches), and more. PJ's Grill (52 Fulham Road, SW3) and Smollensky's (➤ 62) are slightly upscale; Joe Allen (➤ 62) and Christopher's (➤ 62) a lot more so, while Clarke's (124 Kensington Church Street, W8) sits at the top.

AL SAN VINCENZO (££)

Essential to book one of the few tables to enjoy Neapolitan Signore Borgonzolo's cooking.
✚ D5 ✉ 30 Connaught Street, W2 ☎ 0171-262 9623
🕐 Lunch, dinner. Closed Sat lunch, Sun

ARTS THEATRE CAFÉ (£)

Modern Italian cooking at low prices in a basement beneath the theater; head for the set-price menu.
✚ G5 ✉ 6–7 Great Newport Street, WC2 ☎ 0171-497 8014
🕐 Lunch, dinner. Closed Sat lunch, Sun

BERTORELLI'S (££)

Fast becoming a Covent Garden favorite; good buzz and food, and efficient enough to cope with the pre- or post-opera rush from across the way.
✚ G5 ✉ 44a Floral Street, WC2 ☎ 0171-836 3969
🕐 Lunch, dinner. Closed Sun dinner

BOUDIN BLANC (££)

Extremely good-value French food, especially considering its Mayfair setting in Shepherd Market. There's also a cheap pre-8PM menu.
✚ E6 ✉ 5 Trebeck Street, W1 ☎ 0171-499 3292 🕐 Lunch, dinner

CAFÉ DU MARCHÉ (££)

In the cobblestone mews in the square's west corner, this rustic French restaurant has a laid-back pianist each evening.
✚ J4 ✉ 22 Charterhouse Square, EC1 ☎ 0171-608 1609
🕐 Lunch, dinner. Closed Sat lunch, Sun

CHEZ MAX (££)

Head right down to the West Brompton end of Fulham Road for classic French food cooked by the Renzland brothers—at West End prices.
✚ C8 ✉ 168 Ifield Road, SW10 ☎ 0171-835 0874
🕐 Lunch, dinner. Closed Mon lunch, Sun

L'ALTRO (££)

Fashionable Kensington restaurant serving Italian seafood on earthenware platters; much patronized by locals who enjoy the buzz.
✚ A5 ✉ 210 Kensington Park Road, W11 ☎ 0171-792 1066/1077 🕐 Lunch, dinner. Closed Sun dinner

PALAIS DU JARDIN (££)

Good atmosphere and food in a huge designer brasserie, with tables outside in summer.
✚ G5 ✉ 136 Long Acre, WC2 ☎ 0171-379 5353 🕐 Lunch, dinner

PIZZA EXPRESS (£)

Located in a tiled Victorian dairy, a branch of the reliable Pizza Express chain, whose pizzas have thin crispy crusts and good toppings.
✚ G5 ✉ 30 Coptic Street, WC1 ☎ 0171-636 3232
🕐 Lunch, dinner

SPAGHETTI HOUSE (£)

Still Italian-run, this is one of 20 branches in the City serving good pasta, meat and fish at low prices in pleasant surroundings.
✚ F4 ✉ 15–17 Goodge Street, W1 ☎ 0171-636 6582
🕐 Lunch, dinner. Closed Sun lunch

ENGLISH RESTAURANTS

English may be derided as a cuisine, but there is both fine traditional and impressive new wave cooking to be enjoyed, though it is not cheap.

ALASTAIR LITTLE (£££)
The price is high and, because of the plate-glass façade, diners may be gawped at by passers-by, but the food is innovative, even sublime.
➕ F5 ✉ 49 Frith Street, W1 ☎ 0171-734 5183 🕐 Lunch, dinner. Closed Sat lunch, Sun

ATLANTIC BAR AND GRILL (££)
A big, lofty basement in the Regent Palace Hotel off Piccadilly Circus; good bar, which attracts a trendy clientele.
➕ F5 ✉ 20 Glasshouse Street, W1 ☎ 0171-734 4888 🕐 Lunch, dinner. Closed lunch Sat and Sun. Dress code: trendy

THE CONNAUGHT (£££)
Whether you choose the more public restaurant or the pale green Grill Room at the back, all is quintessentially English.
➕ E5 ✉ Carlos Place, W1 ☎ 0171-499 7070 🕐 Lunch, dinner. Dress code: jacket and tie

FRENCH HOUSE DINING ROOM (££)
Cozy dining-room over a Soho pub serves modern dishes. Its Clerkenwell outpost is the St. John.
➕ F5 ✉ 45 Dean Street, W1 ☎ 0171-437 2477 🕐 Lunch, dinner. Closed Sun

THE IVY (££)
A revived theaterland classic with artworks by Peter Blake and Howard Hodgkin on the walls, celebrities galore and modern British food.
➕ G5 ✉ 1 West Street, WC2 ☎ 0171-836 4751 🕐 Lunch, dinner

LEITH'S (£££)
Go for the imaginative modern British food, with plenty of vegetarian dishes, not for the new, sterile décor.
➕ A5 ✉ 92 Kensington Park Road, W11 ☎ 0171-229 4481 🕐 Dinner only

RULES (££)
Founded in 1798, one of London's oldest restaurants serves reliable, traditional food in its plush Edwardian rooms.
➕ G5 ✉ 35 Maiden Lane, WC2 ☎ 0171-836 5314 🕐 Lunch, dinner

SIMPSON'S (££)
This was opened in 1848 as Simpson's Divan and Tavern, where chess players lolled on divans to feast on roast beef. Today, there's just the roast beef and other traditional dishes, including hefty desserts.
➕ G5 ✉ 110 Strand, WC2 ☎ 0171-836 9112 🕐 Breakfast, lunch, dinner. Dress code: jacket and tie

STEPHEN BULL (££)
Stephen Bull's original, rather spartan restaurant delivers robust, modern British food to a serious, appreciative clientele. There's a Bistro branch in Clerkenwell.
➕ E5 ✉ 7 Blandford Street, W1 ☎ 0171-486 9696 🕐 Lunch, dinner. Closed Sat lunch, Sun

Eat as much as you can buffet deals

Unlimited food at a fixed price may be essential for families with growing children—or simply for hungry adults. The Waldorf Hotel's buffet breakfast makes a good start to the day (➤ 64). Many larger hotels, such as the Langham (Langham Place, W1) and Basil Street (➤ 85), do the equivalent but at lunchtime. Sunday lunch buffets in Indian restaurants are fun.

SHOPPING AREAS

London's stores tend to be found in clusters; conserve your energy and shop in one area. Regular store hours are 9:30 or 10AM until between 5:30 and 7PM, with late-night shopping in Knightsbridge on Wednesdays, Oxford Street and Covent Garden on Thursdays.

Tax-free goods

If you are a non-U.K. passport holder, it is worth considering the VAT Retails Export Scheme. VAT (Value Added Tax) is rated at 17½ percent in Britain and payable on almost everything except books, food and children's clothes. All non-U.K. passport holders are exempt from VAT if they are taking the goods out of the country within three months. The tax must be paid first, then claimed back. You must have your passport and return ticket with you; the shop assistant will help you complete the form VAT407—make sure you keep your part of it along with the export sales bill. Show Customs this form and have your goods ready to show.

BOND STREET

Bond Street mixes haute-couture outlets with art galleries. Asprey's, one of the world's great luxury stores, is here, as are the Fine Art Society and Sotheby's.
✚ F5 ✉ Mayfair

BROMPTON CROSS

Sophisticated fashion and design stores. The Conran store, selling quality design, is the longest-established store.
✚ D7 ✉ Knightsbridge/Chelsea, SW3

JERMYN STREET

Once the local street for aristocrats swarming around St. James's Palace; the atmosphere of Jermyn Street remains select: Floris the perfumier (est. 1730); Paxton & Whitfield for cheeses, and Harvie and Hudson or Turnbull & Asser for shirts.
✚ F6 ✉ St. James's, SW1

KENSINGTON CHURCH STREET

This once-quiet lane now has more than 50 antiques stores, Clarke's restaurant (and bakery next door); Boyd's and Kensington Place.
✚ B6 ✉ Kensington, W8

NEAL STREET

The epitome of Covent Garden's successful rebirth, this pedestrian street is packed with exotic little stores: Smith's Gallery, Neal Street East, the Kite Store and, in Neal's Yard, a feast of whole foods.
✚ G5 ✉ Covent Garden, WC2

OLD COMPTON STREET

In the 18th century, this was the social center for French exiles. Pâtisserie Valerie at no. 44 keeps the mood alive; Italians run the tiny Pollo and Presto bars, Vinorio, Camisa and the newsstand Moroni's.
✚ F5 ✉ Soho, W1

OXFORD STREET

The capital's main shopping artery. At the west end, Marks & Spencer stocks the chain's greatest variety of clothing; in the middle are Selfridges and branches of all significant chains from Body Store to Gap, and John Lewis.
✚ E5, F5, G5
✉ Mayfair/Marylebone, W1

REGENT STREET

With its dramatic curve north from Piccadilly, Nash's street is as chic as intended: Tower Records, Austin Reed, the sumptuous Café Royal, Mappin and Webb (silver), Garrard (jewels), Hamleys (toys), Liberty (► 71) and the Warner Bros. and Disney stores. North of Oxford Street lies the excellent B.B.C. store.
✚ F5 ✉ Mayfair/Soho, W1

DEPARTMENT STORES

GENERAL TRADING COMPANY
There are quality buys in all departments from china to gardening and an excellent mail-order catalogue.
✚ E7 ✉ 144 Sloane Street, SW1 ☎ 0171-730 0411

FORTNUM AND MASON
Before going in, do not miss the clock, which has Messrs. Fortnum and Mason mincing forward each hour. Prices are high, but the store-brand goods make perfect presents.
✚ F6 ✉ 181 Piccadilly, W1 ☎ 0171-734 8040

HARRODS
This vast emporium contains just about everything anyone could want, and a dozen restaurants. In addition to 60 fashion departments, do not miss the eight spectacular food halls.
✚ D6 ✉ Knightsbridge, SW1 ☎ 0171-730 1234

HARVEY NICHOLS
This is London's classiest clothes store, from its constantly original store-windows to the well-stocked fashion floors.
✚ E6 ✉ 109–125 Knightsbridge, SW1 ☎ 0171-235 5000

JOHN LEWIS
Its slogan, "never knowingly undersold," inspires a confidence that prices are solidly fair.
✚ F5 ✉ Oxford Street, W1 ☎ 0171-629 7711

LIBERTY
This store's quality stock is characterized by exoticism mixed with an Arts and Crafts heritage. Goods on offer range from sumptuous fabrics to the best china and glass.
✚ F5 ✉ Regent Street, W1 ☎ 0171-734 1234

LILLYWHITES
When the rain comes, this is the place to go and get what you need, either by Aquascutum, or perhaps Barbour, Partridge or Husky; and whatever the sport, this store has the outfit and equipment.
✚ F5 ✉ Piccadilly Circus, W1 ☎ 0171-930 3181

MARKS & SPENCER
Most people buy something at M&S. Adult and children's clothes now have sharper styles, and the food departments are exceptional. No credit cards accepted.
✚ E5 ✉ 458 Oxford Street, W1 ☎ 0171-935 7954

SCOTCH HOUSE
Plaid and more plaid on three floors. Especially good for soft lambswool and cashmere woolens, as well as traditional, quality Scottish clothing.
✚ D6 ✉ 2 Brompton Road, SW1 ☎ 0171-581 2151

SELFRIDGES
The vastness of this store can bedazzle and confuse. It stocks beauty goods available nowhere else, prepared food, and creates Christmas window displays that deserve a special night outing.
✚ E5 ✉ 400 Oxford Street, W1 ☎ 0171-629 1234

One-stop shopping
The one-stop shopping that department stores offer has several advantages over schlepping around the streets. If it rains, you stay dry. If you are hungry, there are cafés. There are also the services to be considered. Your purchases from various departments can be held for you while you shop, to be collected together at the end. Garments can be altered, presents wrapped and writing paper printed. And most stores have dependable after-sales service if something is not right.

ART & ANTIQUES

Buying at auction

Watching an auction is one thing; buying is quite another. At the pre-sale viewing, inspect any lot you may bid for and check its description and estimated sale price in the catalogue. If you cannot attend the sale, leave a bid; if you can, decide on your maximum bid and do not go above it! Bid by lifting your hand up high. If successful, pay and collect after the sale, or arrange for delivery.

ANTIQUARIUS

London's oldest antiques center houses 120 dealers whose goods include lace, old clothes and jewelry; there are plenty of quirky items here, at affordable prices.

✚ D8 ✉ 131–141 King's Road, SW3 ☎ 0171-351 5353

BONHAM'S

The strength of this auction house (still a family firm) lies in its 20th-century and specialist sales. Chelsea Galleries has cheaper goods.

✚ D7 ✉ Montpelier Galleries, Montpelier Street, SW7 ☎ 0171-584 9161

CHRISTIE'S

The auction house has departments ranging from grand Old Masters to coins and tribal art. Second sale room in South Kensington.

✚ F6 ✉ Christie, Manson & Wood, 8 King Street, SW1 ☎ 0171-839 9060

GRAY'S ANTIQUE MARKET

High-quality goods ranging from pictures to silver, from all periods, sold at 170 stalls, all housed in two adjoining buildings.

✚ E5 ✉ 1–7 Davies Mews and 58 Davies Street, W1 ☎ 0171-629 7034

LEGER GALLERIES

Top English paintings and watercolors by artists such as Turner and Gainsborough; Agnew's, Colnaghi, Frost & Reed and Philip Mould near by are also worth visiting.

✚ F6 ✉ 13 Old Bond Street, W1 ☎ 0171-629 3538

MALLETT AT BOURDON HOUSE

Highly polished tables, chairs and other furniture exhibited in the rarefied atmosphere of a 1720s house; well worth visiting.

✚ E5 ✉ 2 Davies Street, W1 ☎ 0171-629 2444

SOTHEBY'S

The world's largest auction house. This is a rabbit-warren of sale rooms with objects of all kinds on view almost continuously.

✚ F5 ✉ 34 New Bond Street, W1 ☎ 0171-493 8080

SPINK & SON

Spink & Son are best known for their coins, medals and ravishing silver and watercolors; see also their Indian and Far Eastern department.

✚ F6 ✉ 5 King Street, SW1 ☎ 0171-930 7888

VIGO CARPET GALLERY

A huge stock from all periods, with helpful staff to make sense of this mysterious subject.

✚ F5 ✉ 6a Vigo Street, W1 ☎ 0171-439 6971

WADDINGTON GALLERIES

In a small street lined with about 20 galleries selling modern art, Waddington is just one worth seeing; try also Theo Waddington, Redfern, the Gallery and Browse & Darby, and explore nearby Clifford and Derring Streets.

✚ F5 ✉ 12 & 34 Cork Street, W1 ☎ 0171-437 8611/439 6262

CHINA & GLASS

Do not worry about breaking your valuable purchases on the way home; they can be packed and sent home for you, fully insured.

ARAM
Aram's international contemporary design includes works by Depadova; the company has a branch in Hampstead, too.
🚇 G5 ✉ 3 Kean Street, WC2 ☎ 0171-240 3933

ARIA TABLE ART
Well worth the pilgrimage to North London to see a varied stock of modern international state-of-the-art design, with plenty of Italian pieces on display.
🚇 H2 ✉ 133 Upper Street, N1 ☎ 0171-226 1021

DESIGNER'S GUILD
Tricia Guild's store is a wonderland of exquisite design. As well as the pieces of contemporary china and glass, you may find her fabrics irresistible.
🚇 D8 ✉ 277 King's Road, SW3 ☎ 0171-351 5775

HABITAT
Founded by Sir Terence Conran, this contemporary furniture store stocks a variety of glass and china.
🚇 F4 ✉ 196 Tottenham Court Road, W1 ☎ 0171-631 3880

HEAL'S
A forerunner of the Arts and Crafts movement in the 1920s, Heal's specialises in timeless modern furniture.
🚇 F4 ✉ 196 Tottenham Court Road, W1 ☎ 0171-636 1666

JEANETTE HAYHURST
This is one of the few places to find old glass, especially British pieces; also stocks interesting studio glass.
🚇 B6 ✉ 32a Kensington Church Street, W8 ☎ 0171-938 1539

REJECT CHINA SHOP
This, the largest branch of the chain, stocks Spode and Denby and plenty of pottery and earthenware, as well as crystal and cutlery.
🚇 D7 ✉ 183 Brompton Road, SW3 ☎ 0171-581 0739

RJ HOME SHOP
This cut-price store always has bargains, especially in glass, but inspect the goods carefully.
🚇 F4 ✉ 209 Tottenham Court Road, W1 ☎ 0171-436 7941

RON ARAD ASSOCIATES
Ron Arad's designs are one-of-a-kind pieces, which often use brass and stainless steel.
🚇 E2 ✉ 62 Chalk Farm Road, NW1 ☎ 0171-284 4963

WATERFORD WEDGWOOD
The largest selection of hand-made, full lead crystal Waterford glass, all made in Ireland, and Wedgwood china. Will phone the factory for special orders, help customers search for designs no longer made and ship goods worldwide.
🚇 F5 ✉ 173–4 Piccadilly, W1 ☎ 0171-629 2614

Silver
English silver is one of the best antiques buys because it has been hallmarked since the mid-17th century, so you know precisely what you are buying. To get a good look, wander the London Silver Vaults in Chancery Lane, Antiquarius (135–41 King's Road, SW3), Gray's Antique Market (➤ 72), Garrard (➤ 70), and Mappin & Webb (➤ 70). Buy there or visit Christine Schell (15 Cale Street, SW3) (for silver and tortoiseshell) and John Jesse (160 Kensington Church Street, W8) (art deco).

STREET MARKETS

Fashion

To buy international high fashion, explore Harvey Nichols (➤ 71) and the stores lining Sloane Street, Brompton Cross, Beauchamp Place, Bond Street, South Molton Street, and St. Christopher's Place. For more dramatic, innovative, streetwise fashion, explore Hyper-Hyper and Kensington Market (both Kensington High Street, W8), then visit Vivienne Westwood (6 Davies Street, W1), American Retro (35 Old Compton Street, W1) and, in Covent Garden, Michiko Koshino (70 Neal Street, WC2), Jones (13 Floral Street, WC2), Space NK (41 Earlham Street, WC2), Sign of the Times (Shorts Gardens, WC2), and Red or Dead (33 Neal Street, WC2).

Smithfield meat market

Smithfields (EC1) is the only large, fresh-food, commercial market left in Central London. Thousands of bloody carcasses hung up on iron hooks are traded in Horace Jones's grand 19th-century building. Trading starts at 5AM and the market closes down at noon (Mon–Fri).

BERMONDSEY MARKET (NEW CALEDONIAN MARKET)

You need to know your stuff here. And as the big dealers and auction house experts get here before dawn, the earlier you go the better.

➕ L7 ✉ Long Lane and Bermondsey Street, SE1
🕐 Fri 5–2 🚇 Borough or London Bridge

BRIXTON MARKET

Best to go on Saturday, when the streets buzz with local African and Caribbean community shoppers buying their mangoes, sweet potatoes, snapper fish, calf's feet, and ready-cooked delicacies.

✉ Brixton Station Road, Electric Avenue and Popes Road, SW9
🕐 Mon–Sat 8–6 (Thu until 1)
🚇 Brixton 🚉 Brixton

CAMDEN MARKETS

The small, vibrant market in Camden Lock has expanded and spawned other markets to fill every patch of space from the Underground station up to Hawley Road. Find crafts, clothes, books and more.

➕ E2 ✉ Camden High Street to Chalk Farm Road 🕐 Sat, Sun 8–6 🚇 Camden Town

CAMDEN PASSAGE

Bargain hard at the large, twice-weekly open-air antiques market held in front of the antiques stores; then try Chapel Street general market across Upper Street.

➕ H3 ✉ Islington N1
🕐 Wed 9–mid afternoon, Sat 9–5 🚇 Angel

GREENWICH MARKET

Hundreds of stalls selling antiques and crafts, clothes, old books and more. A good start to a Greenwich day (➤20).

✉ College Approach, Stockwell Street and corner of High Road and Royal Hill, SE10 🕐 Sat, Sun 9–6 🚉 Greenwich or Island Gardens DLR then walk the tunnel

LEADENHALL MARKET

A surprising City treat housed under Horace Jones's 1880s arcades, with quality butchers, cheesemongers, fish-mongers, etc. plus pubs.

➕ K5 ✉ Leadenhall, EC3
🕐 Mon–Fri 8–4 🚇 Bank or Monument

PETTICOAT LANE MARKET

Originally a Tudor clothes market; Jewish immigration stimulated its growth into Victorian London's largest market; bargain hard for fashion, leather, household goods and knick-knacks. Brick Lane market is near by.

➕ K5 ✉ Middlesex Street, E1
🕐 Sun 9–2 🚇 Aldgate or Aldgate East

PORTOBELLO MARKET

Saturday is the big day, when antiques and not-so-antiques are sold from the stores and the solid line of stalls in front of them. There are lower prices lower down the hill, with second-hand stalls beneath Westway.

➕ B5 ✉ Portobello Road, W11 🕐 Fruit and vegetables Mon–Sat; general Fri 8–3; antiques Sat 8–5 🚇 Ladbroke Grove

MUSEUM & GALLERY SHOPS

BRITISH MUSEUM & BRITISH LIBRARY (➤ 43)
There are currently three stores, all in or around the entrance hall, plus a children's store in the first floor Egyptian galleries; reproductions, own-brand publications and goods, excellent children's projects. Friends of the B.M. get 10 percent off.

DESIGN MUSEUM (➤ 50)
Extensive and immensely chic designer goods, some with high price tags.

MUSEUM OF LONDON (➤ 47)
Good place to browse through books about London and souvenirs.

NATIONAL GALLERY (➤ 39)
Large store in the Sainsbury Wing, particularly good for paper goods and diaries.

NATIONAL PORTRAIT GALLERY (➤ 38)
Surprisingly large store, well-stocked with books on historical figures, plus own-brand children's book projects.

NATURAL HISTORY MUSEUM (➤ 26)
Thousands of dinosaurs to read about, cut out or put on the mantelpiece; plus plenty about the world since then.

POLLOCK TOY MUSEUM (➤ 59)
Cramped but like an Aladdin's cave for children, toys of all prices including Pollock's toy theaters.

QUEEN'S GALLERY & ROYAL MEWS (➤ 32)
The largest selection of publications and memorabilia about (and in a few instances by) the British royal family.

ROYAL ACADEMY (➤ 51)
If you cannot own a work by a Royal Academician, then buy a plate, mug, pen or book specially designed by one for the R.A. store.

ROYAL BOTANICAL GARDENS, KEW (➤ 24)
Large selection of goods and publications, many lavishly illustrated, to keep the most ardent gardener happy.

SCIENCE MUSEUM (➤ 27)
Plenty of scientific books and projects for budding scientists of all ages.

TATE GALLERY (➤ 34)
The annual Tate diary, its pages scattered with reproductions from the Modern and British collections, has become a collector's item; there's also an extensive quality poster collection.

VICTORIA & ALBERT MUSEUM (➤ 28)
It would be possible to do a full-scale Christmas store here, from toys and books to unique crafts; as expected, an enormous quantity of collection-inspired goods. Friends of the V&A get a 10 percent discount.

Specialty shops

Specialty shops come in every shape and size. Stanley Gibbons (399 Strand, WC2) is a philatelist's paradise, while James Smith & Sons (53 New Oxford Street, W1) stocks every kind of umbrella to keep British rain at bay. Other favorites include Christopher Farr (115 Regents Park Road, NW1) (contemporary carpets), the Crafts Council Shop (44 Pentonville Road, N1 and at the V&A ➤ 28), Creativity (45 New Oxford Street, WC1) (needlework materials), Paperchase (213 Tottenham Court Road, W1) and Smythson's (44 New Bond Street, W1) (both stationers). To find the specialty shop you want, use the Yellow Pages telephone directory which is listed by subject.

BOOKS NEW & OLD

Electronic bargains

To Europeans, London prices for electrical goods seem cheap; to Americans they seem expensive. If you know what you want, compare prices up and down Tottenham Court Road for stereos, and look at New Oxford Street too for computers. Micro Anvika, on Tottenham Court Road, is good for hardware, software and CD-Rom. If daunted, go to Selfridges or Harrods (➤ 71)

THE ATRIUM BOOKSHOP
International books and catalogues on all aspects of the fine and applied arts, especially strong on current exhibitions. Atrium is strong on customer service and can obtain any art book or pamphlet provided it is in print.
✚ F5 ✉ 5 Cork Street, W1
☎ 0171-495 0073

BERNARD QUARITCH
Again, best to make an appointment to come to this, the most splendid and serious of the city's antiquarian bookstores.
✚ F5 ✉ 5 Lower John Street, W1 ☎ 0171-734 2983

BOOKS FOR COOKS
Not merely London's, but possibly the world's best selection of books about cooking and cuisine; orders are taken and dispatched worldwide.
✚ A5 ✉ 4 Blenheim Crescent, W11 ☎ 0171-221 1992

DAUNT BOOKS FOR TRAVELLERS
Amid the paneling and stained glass of his 1910 store, James Daunt keeps a large stock of both traevlogues and guides.
✚ E4 ✉ 83 Marylebone High Street, NW1
☎ 0171-224 2295

DILLONS
This is now London's most extensive bookstore; its search service is good and there are many smaller branches around the capital.
✚ F4 ✉ 82 Gower Street, WC1 ☎ 0171-636 1577

FORBIDDEN PLANET
This store contains an amazing selection of fantasy, horror, science fiction, and comic books of all kinds.
✚ G5 ✉ 71–73 New Oxford Street, W1 ☎ 0171-836 4179

HATCHARDS
Opened in 1797; past patrons have included Wellington, Gladstone, and Macaulay. Hatchards still knows how to make book-buying a delicious experience, with well-informed staff in each department.
✚ F6 ✉ 187 Piccadilly, W1
☎ 0171-493 9921

MAGGS BROTHERS
Make your appointment, then step into this Mayfair mansion to find an out-of-print book, a first edition or a rare antiquarian book; erudite staff include the fifth generation of Maggs.
✚ E6 ✉ 50 Berkeley Square, W1 ☎ 0171-493 7160

STANFORD'S
London's largest selection of maps of countries, cities, and even very small towns around the world, together with travel books.
✚ G5 ✉ 12–14 Long Acre, WC2 ☎ 0171-836 1321

ZWEMMER
Art books fill three neighboring bookstores, divided by category. Here, fine art is upstairs, decorative art and architecture downstairs. The branch at 80 Charing Cross Road holds photography and media; 28 Denmark Street keeps East European titles.
✚ G5 ✉ 24 Litchfield Street, WC2 ☎ 0171-240 4158

FOOD & WINE

With so many parks and benches, a picnic makes a good break from sightseeing or shopping. The big stores have some of the most seductive food halls—and they stock wine; see Harrods (➤ 71), Selfridges (➤ 71), Fortnum & Mason (➤ 71) and Marks & Spencer (➤ 71). Old Compton Street (➤ 70) is a food shopper's delight; see also Clarke's (➤ 70) and cafés (➤ 70), that sell their cakes.

BERRY BROS & RUDD

Opened as a grocery store in 1699; the wines here range from popular varietals to specialty madeiras, ports, and clarets. Their own-label bottles are always good value; perfect service.

➕ F6 ✉ 3 St. James's Street, SW1 ☎ 0171-396 9600

THE BLOOMSBURY WINE AND SPIRIT COMPANY

In addition to wines, the strength of this store is its Scottish malt whiskys: there are more than 170 in stock.

➕ G4 ✉ 3 Bloomsbury Street, WC1 ☎ 0171-436 4763/4

CARLUCCIO'S

A designer deli, stocking only the most refined goods, such as truffle oil, black pasta, and balsamic vinegar.

➕ G5 ✉ 30 Neal Street, WC2 ☎ 0171-240 1487

FRATELLI CAMISA

This, with Lina Stores around the corner in Brewer Street, is one of London's best-loved Italian delicatessens.

➕ F5 ✉ 1A Berwick Street, W1 ☎ 0171-437 7120

NEAL'S YARD DAIRY

A temple to the British cheese, where more than 50 varieties from small farms around Britain are ripened to perfection.

➕ G5 ✉ 17 Shorts Gardens, WC2 ☎ 0171-379 7646

ODDBINS

With more than 60 branches in London, Oddbins is strong on quality, range and price.

➕ G5 ✉ 23 Earlham Street, WC2 ☎ 0171-836 6331

LES SPECIALITÉS ST QUENTIN

Mouth-watering and indulgent food worth getting hungry for.

➕ D7 ✉ 256 Brompton Road, SW3 ☎ 0171-225 1664

VILLANDRY

If the few tables at the back of the store are all taken, then buy bread, oil, quiches and pies and make your way to Regent's Park.

➕ E4 ✉ 89 Marylebone High Street, W1 ☎ 0171-224 3799

WILD OATS

Five hundred customers a day explore the three floors of good quality whole and organic food.

➕ B5 ✉ 210 Westbourne Grove, W11 ☎ 0171-229 1063

Wine

Surprisingly, London has the best variety of international wines at the best prices, for, although Britain is not a major wine-producing country, the British like to drink wine. This explains the range, quality, and fiercely competitive prices in the chains (Oddbins, Threshers) and the supermarkets (Sainsbury's, Waitrose, and Tesco). For bulk buying, consider the Majestic Warehouse chain, a reliable wine merchants, or Christie's and Sotheby's regular wine auctions (➤ 72).

THEATER

Theater tips

If you care about where you sit, go in person and peruse the plan. For an evening "Sold out" performance, it is worth lining up for returns; otherwise, try for a matinée. The cheapest seats could be far from the stage or uncomfortable, so take binoculars and a cushion. As for dress, Londoners rarely dress up for the theater anymore; but they do order their intermission drinks before the play starts, and remain seated while they applaud.

Cheap ticket tips

Use the SOLT Half-price Ticket Booth. Preview tickets are cheaper, as are matinée tickets. Get up early and line up for one-day cheap tickets at the RNT. Go with friends and make a party booking at a reduced rate. Ask the National Theatre, RSC, Royal Court and other theaters about cheap tickets; and keep student and senior citizen cards at the ready. Remember, the show is the same wherever you sit!

Theater in London covers a wide range of venues. It is vibrant, varied, and extensive. The following is intended to help theater-goers find the experience they want.

INFORMATION

Time Out, London's weekly entertainment guide, provides an exhaustive list of all theaters, plus reviews. Daily newspapers carry a less complete but totally up-to-date listing, with more reviews. Ticket prices are cheap for fringe, more expensive for West End and very expensive for musicals.

TICKET BUYING

Telephone booking can be done using a credit card, which must be produced when collecting the tickets. If you book without a credit card, you must usually arrive at the theater 40 minutes before curtain up—or else the tickets will be resold. Booking in person means you can see the seating plan, a good idea if you want a good seat in some of London's older theaters; ask for information on leg room and sightlines.

TICKET AGENCIES

Ticketmaster (0171-344 4444) and First Call (0171-497 9977) are both reliable. Some shows have no booking fee, others a small one, and a few rise to 22 percent of ticket price, so ask first. Beware: it is unwise to buy from small agencies, and very unwise to buy from scalpers.

SOLT HALF-PRICE TICKET BOOTH

Each day a limited number of tickets for some West End shows is sold for that day's performance at half price, plus a £1.50 service charge. The rules are: no credit cards; a maximum of four tickets per person, no exchanges or returns.
➕ G5 ✉ Leicester Square, WC2 🕐 Mon–Sat 2:30–6:30; noon–6:30 on matinée days 🚇 Leicester Square or Piccadilly Circus

THE THEATER YEAR

The theaters are never dark. At any one time there will be an average of 45 West End theaters playing a range of musicals, drama, comedy and thrillers, as well as staging opera and dance. See ► 22 for festivals, many with theatrical events. LIFT (the London International Festival of Theater) takes place in July and August in alternate years. The Royal Shakespeare holds an annual festival, often at the Almeida theater.

WEST END THEATERS

The Society of London Theatre (SOLT) represents the owners, managers, and producers of 54 major London theaters. SOLT runs the annual Lawrence Olivier Awards, London's answer to the Tonys, publishes the fortnightly London Theater Guide (free from theaters) and runs a Theater Token scheme (0171-240 8800) and the SOLT Half-price Ticket Booth (see above).

ROYAL NATIONAL THEATRE (RNT)

British and world drama, classics and new plays. Home of the National Theatre company with three performance spaces —the Olivier, the Lyttelton and the Cottesloe. All have several productions in repertory.
✚ H6 ✉ South Bank , SE1 ☎ 0171-633 0880; booking 0171-928 2252; credit card agency First Call (see above); range of cheap ticket deals. 🚇 Embankment or Waterloo 🚈 Waterloo

ROYAL SHAKESPEARE THEATRE

The London home of the Royal Shakespeare Company (RSC), who perform in the Barbican Theatre (level 3) and The Pit (level 1). Some productions are new, others are transferred from Stratford, and there are always several productions running concurrently in repertory. Annual Prom season, backstage tours.
✚ J4 ✉ Barbican Centre, Silk Street, EC2 ☎ 0171-638 4141; recorded info 0171-628 2295; booking 0171-638 8891; credit card booking daily 9–8, 0171 638 8891; range of cheap ticket deals. 🚇 Barbican

MUSICALS

The successful, long-running shows are dominated by the great impresarios. Sir Andrew Lloyd Webber, who restored and owns the Palace Theatre, has staged *Starlight Express*, *Sunset Boulevard*, *Phantom of the Opera* and *Cats*; the latter two were joint ventures with Cameron Mackintosh, who has had great success with his *Les Misérables*.

LONG-RUNNING STALWARTS

Few plays have the sustained, long-running success of the musicals. Most famous is Agatha Christie's *The Mousetrap* at St. Martin's, aiming for its 50th anniversary in 2002. At the Fortune Theatre, *The Woman in Black* began its run in 1989.

OFF–WEST END THEATER

This new category, devised by *Time Out*, honors the fringe theaters that still stage imaginative productions. Look in the listings for the Almeida, the Bush, Donmar Warehouse, Drill Hall, the Gate, Hampstead, ICA, King's Head, Lyric Studio, Riverside Studios, Royal Court, Theatre Royal Stratford East, Tricycle, and the Young Vic.

FRINGE AND PUB-THEATER

The true fringe, or "alternative" theater in London is vibrant, varied, and dotted about all over the capital in more than 35 venues, many of them pubs. Try the following: Etcetera Theatre (at the Oxford Arms pub), the Finborough, Hen & Chickens, Man in the Moon, New End Theatre, Old Red Lion, and the White Bear.

COMEDY

The Comedy Store's huge popularity recently drove it to larger premises. Also try the Hurricane Club, Banana Cabaret, Jongleurs at the Cornet, Comedy Café, Red Rose Cabaret, and Hackney Empire, a restored music hall that holds vaudeville nights.

Where to find out what's on

Time Out, published every Wednesday, lists everything that's on in London by way of entertainment. The Saturday editions of the *Guardian*, the *Telegraph* and *The Times* and, on Sunday, the *Observer*, *Sunday Times* and *Sunday Telegraph* also have full listings.

Open-air theater

If the weather is good, grab a picnic and head for the Open-Air Theatre, Regent's Park (Jun–Sep), Greenwich Old Observatory (Jul–Aug) or Holland Park Theatre (Jun–Aug).

Children's theater

Several theaters stage magical performances year-round. Names to look for in the listings include the Little Angel Marionette Theatre (doyenne of puppet theaters), Polka Children's Theatre and the Unicorn Theatre for Children. Look for children's productions at the National Theatre, the RSC and mainstream theaters, as well as Punch & Judy in Covent Garden Piazza.

CLASSICAL MUSIC, OPERA & BALLET

THE MUSIC YEAR

Runs non-stop. Look for festivals such as the City of London, Spitalfields, Almeida and Hampton Court Palace, and traditions such as the Christmas Oratorios, carol singing in Trafalgar Square and the Easter Passions. The major classic festival is the Proms, a nickname for the Henry Wood Promenade Concerts, held daily at the Royal Albert Hall and elsewhere from mid-July to mid-September, broadcast live nightly on B.B.C. Radio 3.

THE DANCE YEAR

Very lively, with great variety. Highpoints include the Coliseum's summer season, the Royal Ballet's performances at the Royal Opera House and the Nutcracker Suite season at the Royal Festival Hall (Dec–Jan). Other major venues are: Sadler's Wells, the Place, I.C.A., and Riverside Studios. The climax of the year is Dance Umbrella, a world showcase for contemporary dance (Oct–Nov).

THE OPERA YEAR

Grand opera alternates with dance at the Royal Opera House. Cheaper and often more vibrant opera takes place at the larger Coliseum, where performances are in English. In addition, there are visits from Welsh National Opera, Opera North, Opera Factory, and open-air opera in Holland Park and by Kenwood Lake. Glyndebourne Festival Opera, from late May to August, is only a train ride away in Sussex.
✉ Glyndebourne, Lewes Sussex BN8 5UU
☎ 01273 813813

THE MAJOR VENUES

BARBICAN CONCERT HALL
✚ J4 ✉ Barbican Centre, Silk Street, EC2 ☎ 0171-638 4141; recorded info 0171-628 2295; booking 0171-638 8891; credit card booking daily 9–8, 0171 638 8891; range of cheap ticket deals

LONDON COLISEUM
✚ G5 ✉ St. Martin's Lane, WC2 ☎ 0171-632 8300

ROYAL ALBERT HALL
✚ C6 ✉ Kensington Gore, SW7 ☎ Information 0171-589 3203; box office 0171-589 8212

ROYAL OPERA HOUSE
✚ G5 ✉ Covent Garden, WC2 ☎ 0171-240 1066

SADLER'S WELLS THEATRE
✚ H3 ✉ Rosebery Avenue, EC1 ☎ 0171-278 8916

SOUTH BANK
Royal Festival Hall, Queen Elizabeth Hall and Purcell Room.
✚ G6–H6 ✉ South Bank, SE1 ☎ Recorded information 0171-633 0932; box office 0171-928 8800

WIGMORE HALL
✚ E5 ✉ 36 Wigmore Street, W1 ☎ 0171-935 2141

Food with music

The choice is wide (see Jazz, ▶81). There are tea dances at the Waldorf Hotel (▶64). Claridges' cocktails with their Hungarian Quartet are an institution, while a dinner-dance at the Savoy, Ritz and Claridges is opulently romantic (▶84). Smollensky's (▶62), Rock Garden (5–6 The Piazza, Covent Garden, WC2), Deals West (14–16 Foubert's Place, W1), Break for the Border (8 Argyll Street, W1) and Pizza Pomodoro (51 Beauchamp Place, SW3) are altogether more informal. But if the weather is good, do as Londoners do and head for a park (see Music everywhere!, opposite).

JAZZ & PUB MUSIC

There's plenty to choose from. London boasts the greatest concentration of world-class jazz musicians both home-grown and foreign, traditional and contemporary; look for Camden Jazz Week, Capital Jazz Festival, and the Bracknell Festival. The city also vibrates with evening and late-night gigs covering rock, roots, R&B and much more, some found in pubs. For a full and up-to-date list of venues, check in *Time Out*, published every Wednesday.

BULL'S HEAD, BARNES

Seductive combination of good jazz in the friendly village atmosphere of a riverside pub.
🖂 373 Lonsdale Road, SW13
☎ 0181-876 5241

DOVER STREET WINE BAR

Large, candle-lit, popular basement where the music can be jump-jive, jazz, R&B or Big Band and where the food is good.
✚ F6 🖂 8–9 Dover Street, W1 ☎ 0171-629 9813

DUBLIN CASTLE

Friendly pub for enjoying a variety of folk, rock 'n' roll, blues and soul.
✚ F2 🖂 94 Parkway, NW1
☎ 0171-485 1773

HALF MOON

Jolly pub for R&B played by lesser stars, with plenty of audience participation.
🖂 93 Lower Richmond Road, SW15 ☎ 0181-780 9383

JAZZ CAFÉ

Current favorite among the young, buzzes nightly with the widest range of jazz, from soul to rap.
✚ F2 🖂 5 Parkway, NW1
☎ 0171-916 6000

MEAN FIDDLER

Pub popular for its beer and wide variety of music, which is played in the main hall and the smaller Acoustic room.
🖂 22–28a High Street, Harlesden, NW10
☎ 0181-961 5490

PIZZA EXPRESS, SOHO

Quality pizzas and great, often mainstream, jazz in this friendly Soho cellar.
✚ F5 🖂 10 Dean Street, W1 ☎ 0171-437 9595

PIZZA ON THE PARK

More upmarket than its sister, Pizza Express; top foreign names tend to play at one or other venue.
✚ E6 🖂 11 Knightsbridge, SW1 ☎ 0171-235 5550

RONNIE SCOTT'S

One of the world's best known and most loved jazz clubs, run by jazz musicians for jazz lovers.
✚ F5 🖂 47 Frith Street, W1 ☎ 0171-439 0747

STATION TAVERN

Notting Hill pub that is London's hub for all blues acoustic, R&B and folk.
🖂 41 Bramley Road, W10
☎ 0171-727 4053

Pub music

This can be one of the cheapest and most enjoyable evenings out in London, worth the detour to an off-beat location. For the price of a pint of beer (usually a huge choice) you can settle down to enjoy the ambience and listen to some of the best alternative music available in town, from folk, jazz, and blues to R&B, soul and more. Audiences tend to be friendly, loyal to their venue, and happy to talk music.

Music everywhere!

London is full of music. At lunchtime, the best places are churches, where the regular concerts are usually free. Look in *Time Out* listings (➤ 79) for: in the City St. Anne and St. Agnes, St. Olave's; in the West End St. James's, Piccadilly. Cathedral Evensong is mid-afternoon. On Sundays, cathedrals and churches are again best for sacred music. Look for concerts in historic houses, museums and galleries, especially during the City of London Festival (July). Finally, music is played outdoors in the royal parks, Embankment Gardens and elsewhere, but best of all at Kenwood or Marble Hill on summer evenings.

MOVIES & CLUBS

London lacks the range of movie theaters to be found in some other cities and often receives foreign films long after their home release. But there is plenty of independent and late-night cinema, making a good beginning to a night of clubbing. One-night clubbing is strong, advertised either in *Time Out* (➤ 78/9)or at regular venues. For all but the first club suggested, dress streetwise and pay at the door.

Cocktails and bars

Apart from Smollensky's-on-the-Strand (➤ 62) the best bars are in hotels. For New York style try the Savoy's American Bar (➤ 84). For plushness, the Lanesborough (Hyde Park Corner, SW1) and Langham (Langham Place, SW1) are best. For pampering, head for the Savoy's Thames Foyer and Claridge's lounge (➤ 84). To be seen, go to the Dorchester (Park Lane, W1). To be discreet, go to the Connaught (➤ 69). London's best private bar is at Morton's, the Berkeley Square club that offers temporary membership.

CINEMAS

THE BIG SCREENS
The places to see commercial first runs, but prices are high. Biggest screens are Odeon, Marble Arch, Empire, Leicester Square, Odeon, Leicester Square. Beware of old cinemas divided into multi-screen complexes.

THE INDEPENDENTS
Show a mixture of commercial first runs, foreign (subtitled) and off-beat British films. The most sumptuous are the Minema, Lumière, Curzon Mayfair, Barbican, and the Chelsea Cinema; others include the Screen chain, Camden Plaza, Gate, Metro, and Renoir.

NATIONAL FILM THEATRE
Located next to the Museum of the Moving Image, with two cinemas. Its advantages: good programing, silent audiences, film-buff bookstore, riverside restaurant, children's screenings.
🞤 H6 ✉ South Bank, SE1 ☎ 0171-928 3232

REPERTORY
Good for old movies, seasons, double-bills and late nights. Try the Everyman and the Phoenix; knife-edge contemporary at ICA Cinémathèque; variety at the French and Goethe Institutes. Also the Museum of London's "Made in London" series.

CLUBS

ANNABEL'S
One of the world's most fashionable clubs for the not-so-young. Go with a member, and dress up.
🞤 E5 ✉ 44 Berkeley Square, W1 ☎ 0171-629 2350

BORDERLINE
Mill with the music business insiders.
🞤 G5 ✉ Orange Yard, off Manette Street, W1 ☎ 0171 734 2095

BRIXTON ACADEMY
Splendid building, best Friday, Saturday.
✉ 211 Stockwell Road, SW9 ☎ 0171-924 9999

CAMDEN PALACE
Friendly ambience for a bargain night out; indie bands on Tuesdays.
🞤 F2 ✉ 1a Camden High Street, NW1 ☎ 0171-387 0428

EQUINOX DISCOTHEQUE, EMPIRE BALLROOM
The best for an energetic bop on a crowded floor.
🞤 G5 ✉ Leicester Square, WC2 ☎ 0171-437 1446

GARAGE
Bands range from pop to indie; comedy on Fridays.
🞤 H1 ✉ 20–24 Highbury Corner, N5 ☎ 0171-607 1818

GOSSIPS
Young and friendly, with varied theme nights.
🞤 F5 ✉ 69 Dean Street, W1 ☎ 0171-434 4480

THE VENUE
Worth the journey to hear the best indie bands.
✉ 2a Clifton Rise, New Cross, SE14 ☎ 0181-692 4077

SPECTATOR SPORTS

London offers most sports to watch (and play) in or near the city—often merely an Underground ride away. Major events are held on Saturdays and Sundays, and tickets are readily available (see ticket agencies, ► 78–79).

THE MAJOR VENUES

ALL ENGLAND LAWN TENNIS CHAMPIONSHIPS WIMBLEDON

Tennis's top tournament, starting in late June. Enter the ticket ballot or join lines for ticket, except on the last four days.
⊠ All England Lawn Tennis and Croquet Club, Church Road, SW19 ☎ 0181-946 2244
🚇 Southfields

CRYSTAL PALACE NATIONAL SPORTS CENTRE

The major venue for national competitions.
⊠ Ledrington Road SE19 ☎ 0181-778 0131 🚇 Crystal Palace

LORD'S CRICKET GROUND

Marylebone Cricket Club's home (► 60), where Middlesex plays home games, Test (international) cricket and major finals; Sunday league games.
✚ D3 ⊠ St. John's Wood Road, NW8 ☎ 0171-289 8979
🚇 St John's Wood

THE OVAL

Surrey home games and Test cricket; also Sunday league games.
✚ H8 ⊠ Surrey County Cricket Club, The Oval, SE11 ☎ 0171-582 6660 🚇 Oval

ROYAL ALBERT HALL

Grand Victorian building holding 5,000 spectators; boxing, tennis and sumo wrestling events.
✚ C6 ⊠ Kensington Gore, SW7 ☎ 0171-589 8212
🚇 South Kensington

WEMBLEY STADIUM AND ARENA

A vast complex with Stadium, Arena and Conference and Exhibition Centre. Excellent visitors' tours of the Stadium.
⊠ Wembley, Middlesex
☎ 0181-900 1234; tours 0181-902 8833 🚇 Wembley Park

OTHER MAJOR SPORTS

ASSOCIATION FOOTBALL (SOCCER)

To see the FA Cup final (May) at Wembley, pay high prices; alternatively, visit one of the 12 London clubs (Aug–May) such as Arsenal, Chelsea, Fulham, or Tottenham Hotspur.

AUTO RACING

Plenty of action at Brands Hatch in Kent: racing most weekends of the year, usually motorbikes on Saturdays, cars on Sundays.

RUGBY UNION

Tickets for the internationals at Twickenham are scarce; easier to watch the Varsity match (Dec), the Cup Final (Apr–May) or take in a tour game; easier still to watch a game at one of the ten London clubs such as Blackheath or Harlequins.

Participatory sports

London's many parks and open spaces are alive with people playing tennis, bowls, cricket and soccer, or jogging, walking and boating. For more formal sports, Crystal Palace National Sports Centre has comprehensive facilities; but Kensington Sports Centre (Walmer Road, W1), the Oasis (32 Endell Street, WC2), and the Queen Mother Sports Centre (223 Vauxhall Bridge Road, SW1) are more central. For fitness, Barbican Health & Fitness Centre and Broadgate Club (at the Broadgate Centre, ► 54) have good equipment.

Horse-racing

A British obsession, so there are plenty of races near London during the flat season (Mar–Nov) and winter steeple-chasing (Aug–May). On and off-course, betting is legal and well-governed. Daytime races at Newmarket, Epsom, Goodwood and Ascot can be reached by train from London, or take the train out to Windsor or Kempton for a delightful summer evening meeting. Daily newspapers have details of race meetings.

83

LUXURY HOTELS

To be pampered amid sumptuous surroundings may be an essential part of your vacation. London's most luxurious hotels have been built with no expense spared. A single room costs about £200 per night.

Bargain deals

London hotel prices are very high. But quality rooms can be had for bargain prices. Most deluxe and middle-market hotels offer weekend deals throughout the year, to include breakfast, dinner and even theater tickets. The big chains such as Forte, Mount Charlotte Thistle, and Best Western have brochures offering package deals. Newly refurbished hotels usually have incentive prices, and off-season months such as January and February are a buyer's market.

CLARIDGE'S
From the art deco lobby and mirrored dining room to the huge baths and log fires in the corner suites, this is deluxe Mayfair living.
➕ E5 ✉ Brook Street, W1 ☎ 0171-629 8860; fax 0171-499 2210

DUKES
A stone's throw from St. James's Palace, the aristocratic and intimate flavor of an old St. James's mansion is enhanced by the discreet dining rooms reserved for guests.
➕ F6 ✉ 35 St. James's Place, SW1 ☎ 0171-491 4840; fax 0171-493 1264

FOUR SEASONS HOTEL
Formerly called Inn on the Park, this modern hotel may lack period style, but it provides some of the best service in town.
➕ E6 ✉ Hamilton Place, Park Lane, W1 ☎ 0171-499 0888; fax 0171-493 6629

HALKIN HOTEL
Central London's first and, so far, only deluxe hotel built and furnished in contemporary design throughout, with a suitably upmarket Italian restaurant. An ideal location for visits to Knightsbridge and Mayfair.
➕ E6 ✉ 4 Halkin Street, SW1 ☎ 0171-333 1000; fax 0171-333 1100

HYATT CARLTON TOWER
Modern yet opulent, from the lobby flower arrangements to the rooftop health club.
➕ E7 ✉ 2 Cadogan Place, SW1 ☎ 0171-235 1234; fax 0171-235 9129

MERIDIEN PICCADILLY
Residents can use Champneys health club, which fills the basement; French influence in the well-appointed rooms.
➕ F6 ✉ 21 Piccadilly, W1 ☎ 0171-734 8000; fax 0171-437 3574

THE RITZ
Small but sumptuous, with plenty of old style, gilt decor and the great first-floor promenade to London's most beautiful dining room overlooking Green Park.
➕ F6 ✉ Piccadilly W1 ☎ 0171-493 8181; fax 0171-493 2687

SAVOY
Old-style Thameside hotel between the West End and the City; splendid river suites; art deco rooms; health club.
➕ G5 ✉ Strand, WC2 ☎ 0171-836 4343; fax 0171-240 6040

THE STAFFORD
Tucked behind Piccadilly, with an alley through to Green Park, this small, discreet hotel has a similar intimacy to Dukes but its cozy public rooms are open to non-guests.
➕ F6 ✉ 16 St. James's Place, SW1 ☎ 0171-493 0111; fax 0171-493 7121

MID-RANGE HOTELS

BASIL STREET HOTEL
Tucked behind Harrods and full of old-style comforts, favored by discerning Americans.
✚ D7 ✉ Basil Street, SW3 ☎ 0171-581 3311; fax 0171-581 3693

5 SUMNER PLACE HOTEL
Family-owned and run house-hotel, in South Kensington's chic residential area; a dozen rooms, plus a garden.
✚ C7 ✉ 5 Sumner Place, SW7 ☎ 0171-584 7586; fax 0171-823 9962

HAZLITT'S
Right in the heart of Soho; residents in this period house can live a full Soho life and stroll to the major galleries and museums in minutes.
✚ F5 ✉ 6 Frith Street, Soho Square, W1 ☎ 0171-434 1771; fax 0171-439 1524

HOTEL NUMBER SIXTEEN
Long-established champion of the many delightful London house-hotels (converted from four Victorian houses); log fires, walled garden.
✚ C7 ✉ 16 Sumner Place, SW7 ☎ 0171-589 5232; fax 0171-584 8615

MONTAGUE PARK HOTEL
Bloomsbury houses converted into a traditional hotel; terrace and garden.
✚ G4 ✉ 12—20 Montague Street, WC1 ☎ 0171-637 1001; fax 0171-637 2516

REMBRANDT
Large Edwardian hotel ideal for Knightsbridge and South Kensington, with a health club.
✚ D7 ✉ 11 Thurloe Place, SW7 ☎ 0171-589 8100; fax 0171-225 3363

LA RESERVE
In a west London residential area, right by Chelsea Football Club; period house refurbished in contemporary style.
✚ B9 ✉ 422—428 Fulham Road, SW6 ☎ 0171-385 8561; fax 0171-385 7662

ROYAL OVER-SEAS LEAGUE
Central location; garden overlooking Green Park; no-fuss rooms and restaurant; membership open to all British and Commonwealth citizens and members of affiliated clubs worldwide.
✚ F6 ✉ Over-Seas House, Park Place, St. James's Street, SW1 ☎ 0171-408 0214; fax 0171-499 6738

SCANDIC CROWN VICTORIA
The Scandinavian chain is known for high standards of basics with no frills, and especially good beds. The Scandic Crown Nelson Dock, in Docklands, has river views.
✚ F7 ✉ 2 Bridge Place, Victoria, SW1 ☎ 0171-834 8123; fax 0171-828 1099

SHAFTESBURY
Newly refurbished small hotel in Soho.
✚ F5 ✉ 65—73 Shaftesbury Avenue, W1 ☎ 0171-434 4200; fax 0171-437 1717

Expect to pay around £70–100 per night for a single room in mid-range hotels.

Beware of hidden hotel costs
The room price quoted by a hotel may, or may not, include Continental breakfast, full English breakfast and VAT, which is currently 17.5 percent. Since these affect the final bill dramatically, it is vital to check. Also, check the percentage mark-up on telephone calls, which can be high—there may even be charges for using a telephone charge card; and ask about the laundry and pressing service, which can be very slow.

BUDGET ACCOMMODATION

Budget accommodation can cost anywhere between £15 and £40 per night for a single room.

Location is everything

It is well worth perusing the London map to decide where you are likely to spend most of your time. Then select a hotel in that area or accessible to it by Underground on a direct line, without having to change trains. London is vast and it takes time to cross it, particularly by bus and costly taxis. By paying a little more to be in the center and near your activities, you will save on travel time and costs.

Youth hostels

There are seven hostels in Central London (by Oxford Street, in Holland Park, and by St. Paul's Cathedral, for example), so book well ahead.

✉ Youth Hostels Association, Trevelyan House, 8 St. Stephen's Hill, St. Albans, Hertfordshire AL1 2DY

☎ Information 01727-855 215, fax 01727-844126; booking 0171-248 6547; fax 0171-236 7681

Cheap, clean hotel rooms are not plentiful in central London.

BENTINCK HOUSE HOTEL
Family-run and superbly located, just north of Oxford Street and a stone's throw from Oxford Circus.
✚ E5 ✉ 20 Bentinck Street, W1 ☎ 0171-935 9141; fax 0171-224 5903

ELIZABETH HOTEL
Quiet hotel overlooking a large London square, with car-parking facilities.
✚ F7 ✉ 37 Eccleston Square, SW1 ☎ 0171-828 6812; fax 0171-828 6814

FIELDING HOTEL
Right in Covent Garden and across the road from the Royal Opera House, a favorite with publishers, writers and actors.
✚ G5 ✉ 4 Broad Court, Bow Street, WC2 ☎ 0171-836 8305; fax 0171-497 0064

INTERNATIONAL STUDENTS HOUSE
Rooms and family flats, ideally located right by Regents Park. Book well ahead.
✚ F4 ✉ 229 Great Portland Street, W1 ☎ 0171-631 8300; fax 0171-631 8315

LONDON HOMESTEAD SERVICES
If you want to stay with a London family, this agency has 200 homes to choose from, all within 20 minutes of Piccadilly. There's a minimum 3-night stay.
✉ Coombe Wood Road, Kingston-upon-Thames, Surrey KT2 7JY ☎ 0181-949 4455; fax 0171-549 5492

MANZI'S
Simple rooms above a popular fish restaurant, in an area that buzzes with life day and night.
✚ G5 ✉ 1 & 2 Leicester Street, Leicester Square, WC2 ☎ 0171-734 0224; fax 0171-437 4864

SWISS HOUSE HOTEL
Comfortable little hotel in a pretty residential area of South Kensington.
✚ C8 ✉ 171 Old Brompton Road, SW5 ☎ 0171-373 2769; fax 0171-373 4983

UNIVERSITY WOMEN'S CLUB
Two dozen rooms in an old Mayfair house; membership open to all women graduates and similarly qualified women; friends pay a temporary membership fee.
✚ E6 ✉ 2 Audley Square, South Audley Street, W1 ☎ 0171-499 2268; fax 0171-499 7046

WANSBECK GARDEN HOTEL
Family-owned hotel in an old Bloomsbury house.
✚ G4 ✉ 4–6 Bedford Place, WC1 ☎ 0171-636 6232; fax 0171-831 9170

WHITEHALL HOTEL
Simple, but well-located for Covent Garden and Soho, with a big backyard for relaxing.
✚ G4 ✉ 2–5 Montague Street, WC1 ☎ 0171-580 5871; 0171-323 0409

WINDERMERE HOTEL
Friendly atmosphere and elegant style.
✚ F8 ✉ 142–144 Warwick Way, SW1 ☎ 0171-834 5163; fax 0171-630 8831

LONDON
travel facts

Arriving & Departing

Before you go

- Check that your passport is valid for the whole length of your stay.
- Passport holders from E.U. member countries, the U.S. and some Commonwealth countries (such as Australia and Canada) do not require a visa; visitors from any other country should check.
- Write to London Tourist Board for a free information pack: ✉ 26 Grosvenor Gardens, London, SW1.

When to go

- The tourist season is year-round, and almost all attractions remain open most days of the year.
- High season is Jun–Sep: arrive with a hotel reservation and pre-booked theater seats.
- Quietest months are Jan and Feb. Tickets are easier to find Mon–Thu throughout the year.

Climate

- Officially, London is warmish in summer and coldish in winter, without extremes.
- Officially, London's rainfall is even throughout the year, rising in Sep and Nov.
- Unofficially, London's weather is unpredictable. It may be unusually mild in winter or cold in summer, and it can rain at any time. It is best to dress in layers to overcome temperature changes, and always bring a raincoat.

Arriving by air

- Most London visitors arrive via one of London's five airports:

Gatwick

- Gatwick (☎ 01293 535353, 24 hours) is 50 km (30 miles) south of Hyde Park Corner.

- Two terminals, North and South, each with information desks.
- Trains leave from South Terminal: the Intercity Gatwick Express to Victoria Station (30 minutes) or a Thameslink train via London Bridge, Blackfriars, and City Thameslink to King's Cross station.
- Bus services include Flightline 777, from each terminal to Victoria Coach Station (at least an hour).

Heathrow

- Heathrow is 25 km (15 miles) west of Hyde Park Corner.
- ☎ 0181-745 7702 for Terminal 1—mostly British and Continental flights; ☎ 0181-745 7115 for Terminal 2—mostly Continental; ☎ 0181-745 7412 for Terminal 3—mostly intercontinental; ☎ 0181-745 4540 for Terminal 4—mostly British Airways, intercontinental, Concorde and BA's Paris and Amsterdam flights.
- All four terminals have information desks; London Tourist Board's desk is at Terminals 1, 2, and 3 Underground Station.
- Quickest way to London is by Underground: the two stations, one for Terminals 1, 2 and 3 and one for Terminal 4, are on the Piccadilly line and go direct to Central London (South Kensington 40 minutes, King's Cross 50 minutes).
- Bus services include the two Airbus routes, A1 and A2, from all terminals to several places in London.
- A taxi (usually black) from the official taxi rank will cost more than £30, even outside rush hours.

London City Airport

- ☎ 0171-474 5555. Located beside the City, so use a taxi or the two Airbus shuttles—to Canary Wharf

for Docklands Light Railway or to Liverpool Street Station for the Underground.
• Designed for the business traveler; check-in time is 15 minutes before the flight.

London Luton
• ☎ 01582 405100. Located 53 km (33 miles) north of Central London.
• Mainly U.K. and Continental flights.
• Luton Railway Station is on the Thameslink to King's Cross; buses go to Victoria Coach Station.

Stansted
• ☎ 01279 680500. Located 50 km (30 miles) northeast of Central London.
• Mostly European flights.
• Stansted Express trains run to Liverpool Street Station (40 minutes).

Arriving by sea and train
• The quickest way to London from any port is usually by train, and the cheapest is often by bus.

Arriving via the Channel Tunnel
• Eurostar trains (☎ 01233 617575) are for foot passengers only. Best to book. Trains run between Waterloo International and Paris (3 hours) or Brussels (3 hours 15 minutes), early morning to late at night.
• Le Shuttle (☎ 01900 353535) is for vehicles only. No need to book. Three times an hour between Calais and Folkestone (join the M20 to London at junction 11a), 24 hours a day.

Arriving by car
• Driving in London is slow, parking is expensive and fines are high. Use public transportation.

• Check with your hotel about off-street parking.

Arriving by bus
• Victoria Coach Station
  ✉ Buckingham Palace Road, SW1
  ☎ 0171-823 6567 (information); 0171-730 3499 (Access and Visa bookings).

Customs regulations
• No limit to goods for personal use brought by visitors from E.U. member countries.
• Limits apply for other visitors; if in doubt use the red customs channel.

Departure/airport tax
• This is £10 and is often included in the ticket price.

ESSENTIAL FACTS

Tourist information centers
Main centers
• ✉ Victoria Forecourt, SW1 ◷ Daily 8–7 (Nov–Easter Sun 9–4). The largest center, with comprehensive London information, hotel booking service and bookstore. Free maps for roads, buses and Underground, plus events sheets.
• ✉ Heathrow Terminals 1, 2 and 3 Underground Station Concourse, Heathrow Airport ◷ Daily 8:30–6.
• ✉ Liverpool Street Underground Station, EC2 ◷ Mon 8:15–7, Tue–Sat 8:15–6, Sun 8:30–4:45.
• ✉ Selfridges Basement Services Arcade, 400 Oxford Street, W1 ☎ 0171-629 1234 ◷ Store hours— usually 9:30–7, Thu 9:30–8.

Local centers
• City of London Information Centre ✉ St. Paul's Churchyard, EC4 ☎ 0171-332 1456. ◷ Daily

9:30–5 (Oct–Mar, Sat, Sun
9:30–12:30). Detailed information
on the City of London.
- Greenwich Tourist Information
Centre ✉ 46 Greenwich Church
Street, Greenwich, SE10
☎ 0181-858 6376. ⏰ Daily
10:15–4:45.
- Richmond Tourist Information
Centre ✉ Old Town Hall,
Whittaker Avenue, Richmond,
Surrey ☎ 0181-940 9125
⏰ Mon–Fri 10–6, Sat 9–5
(May–Oct, Sun 10:15–4:15).
- Southwark Tourist Information
Centre ✉ Lower Level, Cottons
Centre, Middle Yard, SE1
☎ 0171-357 9294 ⏰ Mon–Fri
11–5:30; Sat, Sun noon–5:30.
- Twickenham Tourist Information
Centre ✉ The Atrium, Civic
Centre, York Street, Twickenham,
Middlesex ☎ 0181-891 7272
⏰ Mon–Fri 9–5:15.

Visitorcall
- Around-the-clock recorded
telephone guide (⏰ 0839 123456)
covering more than 30 subjects.
Premium rates are charged. To
access specific lines directly, dial
0839 123 plus 400 (what's on this
week), 401 (annual events), 403
(exhibitions), 407 (Sundays in
London), 411 (Changing the
Guard), 416 (popular West End
shows), 424 (where to take
children), 428 (street markets), 429
(museums) or 430 (traveling in
London).

Hotel reservations
- The LTB (☎ 0171-824 8844)
publishes an annual hotel guide,
Where to Stay in London, and runs a
hotel booking service.

British Tourist Authority
- British Travel Centre ✉ 12
Regent Street, Piccadilly Circus,

SW1 (no ☎) ⏰ Mon–Fri 9–6:30,
Sat, Sun 10–4 (May–Sep Sat 10–5).
- British Tourist Authority
Telephone information service
☎ 0181-846 9000.

Opening hours
- Major attractions: seven days a
week, but some open late on Sun.
- Stores: six days a week; some open
on Sun. Late-night shopping until
about 8PM in Knightsbridge on
Wed, and in Oxford and Regent
streets on Thu.
- Banks: Mon–Fri 9:30–5; a few
remain open later or open on Sat
mornings. Bureaux de change have
longer opening hours (including
weekends).
- Post offices: usually Mon–Fri
9–5:30, Sat 9–12:30.

National holidays
- Jan 1; Easter Mon; first Mon in
May; last Mon in May; last Mon in
Aug; Dec 25; Dec 26.
- Almost all attractions close on
Christmas Day. Some stores,
restaurants (particularly in hotels)
and attractions remain open on
other holidays.

Money
- 100 pence to £1. Coins: 1p, 2p, 5p,
10p, 20p, 50p and £1; bills: £5, £10,
£20 and £50.
- Banks often offer a better
exchange rate than *bureaux de
change*. Check rates, commission,
and any other charges.

Tipping
- 10 percent for restaurants, taxis,
hairdressers and other services.
Look over restaurant checks to see
whether or not service charge has
already been added.
- No tipping in theaters, cinemas,
concert halls or in pubs and bars
(unless there is waitress service).

Places of worship
- Almost every denomination is represented. Use the London telephone directory to contact your church headquarters.

Student travelers
- Student or I.S.I.C. cards reduce costs for most attractions, theaters and travel dramatically. Students enrolling for study in London can apply to their union for a card.
- The Young Person's Rail Card reduces fares for anyone aged 16–25 (on sale at main line stations; requires proof of date of birth and two photographs).

Time
- G.M.T. (Greenwich Mean Time) is standard time; clocks move one hour ahead in B.S.T. (British Summer Time: late March to late October).

Toilets
- The cleanest are inside attractions (free); the assistant should receive a small tip.

Electricity
- The E.U. standard supply of 230V applies, with a permitted range of 216.2–253V.
- Motor-driven equipment needs a specific frequency; the U.K. frequency is 50 cycles per second (kHz).

Lone travelers
- Stay near other people on Underground trains and buses, especially at night.
- Keep to well-lit streets; consider buying a personal alarm.
- Avoid minicabs picking up on the street. Hail a black cab. Women traveling alone may like to use Lady Cabs (☎ 0171-254 3314/923 2266).

PUBLIC TRANSPORTATION

London transport travel information centers
- Centers sell travel passes and provide Underground and train maps, bus route maps, and information on cheap tickets.
- Open daily inside following stations: Victoria, Euston, King's Cross, Liverpool Street, Oxford Circus (except Sun), Piccadilly Circus, and St. James's Park (except Sun); also located at each terminal at Heathrow Airport and at Heathrow Terminals 1, 2 and 3 Underground Station.
- London Transport Enquiries telephone service: ☎ 0171-222 1234, 24 hours; 0171-222 1200, travel-check directory, with latest information accessed on any push-button tone-dialing telephone.

Travel passes
- Priced according to length of validity and how many of the six London zones it covers, a pass usually pays for itself within two or three journeys. There are three main types.
- Travelcards: valid after 9:30AM for unlimited travel by Underground, British Rail, Docklands Light Railway, and most buses; on sale at travel information centers, British Rail stations, all Underground stations and some stores (such as newspaper shops); cover travel for one day, a week, a month or a year. Adults need a photocard (except for a one day Travelcard), on sale at travel information centers; children aged 5–15 pay child fares but need a child-rate photocard; children under five travel free.
- Bus passes: bus-only passes are on sale at travel information centers,

Underground stations, and some newspaper shops.

- Visitor Travelcards: similar to Travelcards but no need for a photo; valid for one, three, four or seven days. Must be bought before arrival in London.

The Underground

- Eleven color-coded lines link 273 stations. Use a travel pass (► 91), or buy a ticket from a machine (some give change) or at a ticket booth; keep the ticket until the end of the journey. The system includes the Docklands Light Railway (DLR; runs between Tower Gateway station and the Isle of Dogs).

Buses

- Plan your journey using the latest copy of the *All London Bus Guide*.
- A bus stop is indicated by a red sign on a metal pole.
- On a two-man bus, the conductor comes to inspect the travel pass or sell a ticket; on a one-man bus, the driver inspects passes or sells tickets as passengers board—try to have exact change.

Taxis

- Drivers of official (mostly black) cabs know the city well. They are obliged to follow the shortest route unless an alternative is agreed.
- Hail only taxis with the yellow "For Hire" light on; tell the driver the destination before getting in. A taxi is licensed to take up to four people.
- Meter charges increase in the evenings and on weekends.
- Avoid minicabs; they may have no meter and inadequate insurance.
- Black cabs can be ordered by telephone: Computer Cab (☎0171-286 0286/2728/7272), Radio Taxis (☎0171-272 0272).

MEDIA & COMMUNICATIONS

Telephones

- There are two systems: British Telecom (BT) and its rival, Mercury, which is cheaper for international calls and phonecards.
- Information ☎192.
- Check the mark-up rate before making a call from a hotel.
- Use either coins or a BT phonecard from BT public telephone booths. Phonecards are on sale at post offices and news-stands. Some phone booths take credit cards.
- Emergencies: ☎999 (free) from any telephone for police, fire, or ambulance.
- ☎100 to check costs, reverse charges (call collect) or call person to person within the U.K.
- International telephoning: ☎153 for Directory Enquiries; 155 to reverse the charges.
- Beware of high charges on premium numbers—such as those prefixed 0839 or 0898.

Sending a letter or a postcard

- Stamps are sold at post offices and some newsstands and stores.
- Trafalgar Square Post Office stays open till late: ✉ William IV Street, WC2 🕐 Mon–Sat 8–8.
- Mailboxes are red.

Newspapers

- Quality dailies include *The Times*, the *Financial Times*, the *Daily Telegraph*, the *Independent* and the *Guardian*; Sat editions carry advertisements for concerts.
- Sunday quality papers include the *Sunday Telegraph*, *Observer*, *Sunday Times*, the *Independent on Sunday*.
- London's only evening paper is the *Evening Standard* (Mon–Fri), first edition out around noon. It is

strong on entertainment and
nightlife information.

Magazines

- *Time Out*, published weekly on
  Wed, lists almost everything going
  on in the city.
- The *Radio Times* and *TV Time*s
  provide exhaustive listings for
  television and radio.

Radio

- British radio is high-quality and
  varied.
- Stations include: B.B.C. Radio 3
  (91.3FM: classical music); B.B.C.
  Radio 4 (93.5FM: news, arts);
  B.B.C. World Service (463m/
  648kHzMW: diverse programs,
  world outlook); Capital FM
  (95.8FM: current hit music);
  Choice FM (96.9FM: soul and
  dance music); Classic FM
  (100.9FM: popular classical music);
  Jazz FM (102.2FM: 24-hour jazz).

Television

- B.B.C. 1 (varied programming).
- B.B.C. 2 (more cultural).
- I.T.V. (commercial, varied).
- Channel 4 (commercial, cultural
  and minority interest).
- Satellite and cable channels
  (mainly in larger hotels) include
  CNN, MTV, Sky and a wide range
  of specialty channels.

International newsagents

- A Moroni & Son ✉ 68 Old
  Compton Street, W1 ☎ 0171-437
  6442.
- Pages News ✉ Buckingham
  Palace Road, by Victoria Palace.

EMERGENCIES

Sensible precautions

- Do not wear valuables that can be
  snatched. If you must bring

valuables, put them in a hotel or
bank safe box.
- Carry only a small amount of cash
  and keep it (and your credit cards)
  out of sight.
- Make a note of all passport, ticket,
  and credit card numbers and keep
  it in a separate place.
- Keep money, passport, and credit
  cards in a fully closed bag.
- Keep your bag in sight at all
  times—do not sling it over your
  back or put it on the floor of a café,
  pub, or cinema. Keep an eye on
  your coat, hat, umbrella and
  shopping bags.
- At night, try not to travel alone; if
  you must, either pre-book a taxi or
  keep to well-lit streets and use a
  bus or Underground train where
  there are already other people.

Lost property

- At an airport: Gatwick ☎ 01293
  503162; Heathrow ☎ 0181-759
  4321; London City ☎ 0171-474
  5555; Luton ☎ 01582 405100;
  Stansted ☎ 01279 662520.
- In a British Rail train: telephone
  the mainline station—for example:
  Liverpool Street ☎ 0171-922 9189,
  Victoria ☎ 0171-922 6216,
  Waterloo ☎ 0171-922 6135.
- In an Underground train: Lost
  Property Office 200 Baker Street,
  NW1 ☎ 0171-486 2496.
- In a bus ☎ 0171-222 1234.
- In a taxi 15 Penton Street, N1
  ☎ 0171-833 0996.

Lost credit cards

Report any loss immediately to the
relevant company (so credit can be
stopped) and to the nearest police
station; also telephone your bank.
- Access Nat West ☎ 01532 778899.
- Access Lloyds ☎ 0800 585300.
- American Express ☎ 0171-222
  9633.
- Barclaycard/Visa ☎ 01604 230230.   93

- Diners Club ☎ 01252 513500.
- MasterCard/Eurocard ☎ 01702 362988.

Medical treatment

- E.U. nationals and citizens of some other countries with special arrangements (e.g., Australia and New Zealand) may receive free National Health Service (NHS) medical treatment while in the U.K. Others must pay for everything.
- If you need an ambulance ☎ 999 on any telephone, free of charge.
- National Health Service hospitals with 24-hour emergency departments include: University College Hospital Gower Street (entrance in Grafton Way), WC1 ☎ 0171-387 9300; Chelsea and Westminster Hospital 369 Fulham Road, SW10 ☎ 0171-746 8000.
- Private hospitals, with no emergency unit, include the Cromwell Hospital, Cromwell Road, SW5 ☎ 0171-370 4233.
- Great Chapel Street Medical Centre 13 Great Chapel Street, W1 ☎ 0171-437 9360 is an NHS clinic open to all, but visitors from countries without the NHS reciprocal agreement must pay.
- Dental specialist: Eastman Dental Hospital, 256 Gray's Inn Road, WC1 ☎ 0171-837 3646; 24 hours.
- Eye specialists: Moorfields Eye Hospital, City Road, EC1 ☎ 0171 253 3411; 24 hours; First Sight Opticians, 229–31 Regent Street, W1 ☎ 0171-499 8777. Optician and on-site workshop for glasses and contact lenses.
- For homeopathic chemists, practitioners and advice: the British Homeopathic Association, 27a Devonshire Street, W1 ☎ 0171-935 2163; The Royal London Homeopathic Hospital,

Great Ormond Street, WC1 ☎ 0171-837 3091.

Medicines

- Britain has a very cautious drugs policy, and many cannot be bought over the counter. For an NHS prescription, the pharmacist is paid a modest flat rate; if a private doctor prescribes, you pay the full cost. To claim charges back later on insurance, keep receipts.

Drug stores open late include:
- Bliss Chemist, 5 Marble Arch, W1 ☎ 0171-723 6116. ⊙ Daily 9AM–midnight.
- Ainsworth's Homeopathic Pharmacy, 38 New Cavendish Street, W1 ☎ 0171-935 5330. ⊙ Mon–Fri 9–5:30, Sat 9–4.

Emergency telephone numbers

- For police, fire, or ambulance, ☎ 999 from any telephone, free of charge. The call goes directly to the police, fire, and ambulance services. It is important that you can tell the operator which street you are on and the nearest landmark, intersection or house number; stay by the telephone until the service arrives.

Embassies and consulates

- Australian High Commission, Australia House, Strand, WC2 ☎ 0171-379 4334.
- Canadian High Commission, Macdonald House, 1 Grosvenor Square, W1 ☎ 0171-258 6600.
- Irish Embassy, 17 Grosvenor Place, SW1 ☎ 0171-235 2171.
- New Zealand High Commission, New Zealand House, 80 Haymarket, SW1 ☎ 0171-930 8422.
- Embassy of the United States of America, Grosvenor Square, W1 ☎ 0171-499 9000.

INDEX

ACKNOWLEDGEMENTS

The Automobile Association would like to thank the following photographers,
libraries and associations for their assistance in the preparation of this book.
© BRITISH MUSEUM 43 COURTAULD INSTITUTE GALLERIES 41
NATIONAL PORTRAIT GALLERY 38a, 38b REX FEATURES LTD 9
SCIENCE MUSEUM 27 SPECTRUM COLOUR LIBRARY 13b, 29, 32
All remaining pictures are held in the Association's own library (AA PHOTO
LIBRARY) with contributions from: P BAKER 7, 45b; D FORSS 2; S & O
MATHEWS 46b; R MORT 13a, 18, 48b, 54, 61a; B SMITH 24a, 24b, 30b, 35a,
40a; R STRANGE 6, 23b, 25, 26a, 26b, 28a, 28b, 30a, 31, 44, 46a, 47, 49a, 49b,
50, 58, 60, 87b; M TRELAWNY 16, 21, 42a, 56; R VICTOR 23a; W VOYSEY 1,
12, 17, 33b, 35b, 36, 40b, 48a, 57; P WILSON 5a, 39, 53, 87a; T WOODCOCK
33a, 34, 37b, 45a, 55.

Copy-editors: *Celia Woolfrey, Nia Williams*
Verifier: *Lucy Koserski*
Indexer: *Marie Lorimer*
Original design: *Design FX*